From
Train Set
to
Model Railway

From
Train Set
to
Model Railway

Chris Hatton

Ian Allan PUBLISHING

**In fond memory of Bev Trenberth,
a truly extraordinary person and a true friend.**

First published 2009

ISBN 978 0 7110 3382 5

Published by Ian Allan Publishing

an imprint of Ian Allan Publishing Ltd, Hersham, Surrey, KT12 4RG
Printed in England by Ian Allan Printing Ltd, Hersham, Surrey, KT12 4RG

Code: 0909/B2

Visit the Ian Allan Publishing website at www.ianallanpublishing.com

Contents

Introduction

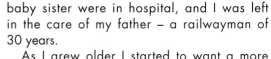

Right: A GWR '45xx' exits the tunnel at the end of Gorran and heads for the station.

Below: A Southern Railway passenger working heads out over the viaduct at the end of Gorran. This viaduct was constructed from a cardboard kit, as described in Chapter 8.

I recall the train sets of my youth extremely clearly, and with very fond memories. Whole days at weekends and during school holidays were spent arranging and rearranging my substantial collection of track and cardboard buildings into ever more complicated layouts. I think that the most exciting thing I recall about the birth of my sister was the fact that I was allowed to leave my train set all over the lounge *and* dining room floors overnight (a previously unheard of occurrence!) while my mother and baby sister were in hospital, and I was left in the care of my father – a railwayman of 30 years.

As I grew older I started to want a more permanent home for the model railway stations I was creating, so that I would not have to demolish them every evening in order to pack them away. I started to wish I had a base on which I could set out the track and buildings permanently so that I could concentrate my spare time on creating models of some of the features and landscapes found around railway lines. What I desired, in fact, was a model railway – something I have defined in the loosest sense here as a landscape created in miniature on a permanent baseboard (rather than the living room floor) through which a substantial amount of railway can run.

This book describes the transition from train set to model railway. It is a journey which an increasing number of people are making, particularly with the recent resurgence of model-railway building; a result perhaps of the dramatic increase in the quality of model trains produced around the turn of the millennium. I hope this book will be of use to all people setting out on the task of constructing a model railway for the first time. I also hope that it will help those who have already laid some track on a baseboard, but are wondering how to progress towards some of the extremely impressive model railways (also sometimes called layouts) which can be seen at railway exhibitions and in railway magazines today. It discusses the major tasks involved and considers how to avoid some of the pitfalls which could be encountered along the way.

The following chapters are arranged so that each deals with a particular aspect of model railway construction. The progression from chapter to chapter charts the progress of a model railway, from building the first baseboard through to adding the finishing touches to the final model. Each chapter discusses a range of approaches to a variety of problems, the simplest usually being addressed first.

Generally, this book considers constructing things from kits and it does not discuss at length the world of fine-scale modelling, where precise models of particular prototypes are constructed from scratch from base materials like brass or plastic sheet. Most chapters do, however, end with a fleeting glimpse of this world to whet the appetite of the modeller who has mastered the techniques described here. It is hoped that these glimpses will not discourage the modeller from laying his first piece of track on his first baseboard, which is by no means the intention. In fact, a huge amount of potential enjoyment building your first model railways would be lost were you to jump straight into fine-scale

modelling. Readers requiring detailed descriptions of fine-scale modelling techniques are directed towards the publications listed in the 'Recommended Reading' section at the end of this book.

This book covers quite a bit of ground, and you may feel somewhat daunted after your first flick through the pages, believing that you are going to have to master electrical circuit construction and all manner of similarly unpalatable-sounding skills to be able to build a model railway. This is not the case at all. I have included such items here to provide a comprehensive overview; a book which will be of use to railway modellers over a period of years as they develop their layouts into ever more convincing representations of the real thing. There is absolutely no need to be entirely confident from the outset with every technique described in these pages.

The book is written chiefly with models of the railways of Great Britain in mind, and suitable kits are recommended for this purpose. However, the techniques described would be equally applicable to a model representing almost any railway system in the world; a baseboard is a baseboard, whatever colour the trains running on it are painted.

The majority of the photographs in this book (particularly those showing models in the course of construction) have been taken during the construction of part of a layout called Gorran.

Left: Time can be spent detailing model railways in a way which is rarely, if ever, achieved with a train set. Scenes such as this can therefore be created, including a wealth of small touches such as the signs on the wall or the lamps resting on the buffer-stops. Once a few of the highly detailed trains available these days are placed on the layout, an extremely realistic model can be created. This is Clunderwen, West Wales, in 1960. *A. Attewell*

Right: A stopping passenger service clanks over the small road bridge at the end of the station at Gorran. The locomotive is a good example of the standard of ready-to-run model which can be bought today.

This is a fictitious Southern Region station loosely modelled to represent the early 1950s. It is probably on a secondary double-track route somewhere in Sussex (the Arun valley is vaguely in my mind as a location), although the station itself is entirely a product of my imagination and the name has been stolen from a village in Cornwall. Although the complete plan for the model railway is shown in Chapter 2, the photographs only cover the construction of the two baseboards at the right hand end of the layout – you will search in vain for photographs of the junction, the goods shed or the platforms. The construction of the part of the layout shown here has been somewhat accelerated to meet the programme for this book. The rest will no doubt follow at a more leisurely pace, during occasional evenings and at weekends, which is the beauty of having a model railway constructed on a baseboard. It can be brought out and put away whenever convenient to the modeller, and no time is lost setting everything out again, as was the case with my train set.

Acknowledgements

The writing of this book would quite definitely have been impossible without considerable help from a number of people.

Had Kevin Robertson not published my last book about garden railways, the chance conversation that we had after that project about the idea of writing this one would never have happened. I am also indebted to Kevin for his generosity in relinquishing what was really his idea for a book, which kick-started the project with Ian Allan, and for putting me in contact with Austin Attewell, who has kindly allowed me to use some of his fantastic collection of photographs within these pages.

A Herculean effort was made by Victoria McIntosh, reading through my initial drafts and transforming my rather roughly hewn words into much more finely fettled chapters. I know, from correcting my chapters with her marked-up prints, just how much work must have been involved in this process, and I am extremely grateful to her.

My father – modeller and railwayman *extraordinaire* – has been unendingly helpful during this project, assisting me both by checking the text for factual errors and by modelling during days and evenings when he thought he was coming down for a holiday with us in Cornwall. A few feet of retaining wall was produced at immense speed one evening towards the end of the project, and the pesky job of lining up all the smokejacks on the engine shed roof was taken from me, which was extremely welcome at the time! The track plans and wiring diagrams within these pages are also the product of his Western Region-trained drawing hand, and I could not hope to have done the job to such a high standard myself. He also took a number of photographs of his own London & South Western Railway epic 'Yes Tor Junction', which can be seen throughout this book.

My mother has, again, waded through pages and pages of drafts correcting my terrible use of commas and split infinitives, and provided words and postcards of encouragement as the deadline drew nearer and nearer. For both of these tasks I am very thankful.

The people at Ian Allan have been encouraging and helpful throughout, which is just what an author needs as he is slogging away at a text, and I am also grateful to my relative David Allen for letting me take photographs of his 'OO' layout 'Casterbridge', which I have always found a very enjoyable and well-thought-through layout to operate. I must thank my friend Andy Waterman for his photographical help, which saved me a lot of time when I didn't have any spare at all. My sister Bryony also deserves my thanks for understanding why there had to be a temporary pause in her open invitation to stay at ours at weekends.

I would also like to acknowledge the Kernow Model Rail Centre in Camborne, who always answering my increasingly frantic phone calls politely and helpfully. It is through them that almost all of the components shown within these pages have been purchased.

To all of the above, a heartfelt thankyou.

Chris Hatton
St Erney, Cornwall
June 2009

1 A History of the Prototype

Right: A model of a London & South Western Railway locomotive resplendent in its original pre-Grouping colours heads over the viaduct into Yes Tor Junction.

The world's first steam locomotive was constructed in this country in 1804 by Richard Trevithick. It was called the *Penydarren* engine and was built to haul coal along a tramway in the Welsh Valleys. This was rapidly followed by other experimental types of locomotive, including the famous *Rocket*, constructed by George Stephenson for the opening of the Liverpool & Manchester Railway in 1830. Such was the success of this line that a period of 'Railway Mania' followed in the mid-1840s when investors poured money into the construction of around 6,000 miles of railway, which constitutes much of the modern railway map.

The late 19th century saw a period of consolidation, many small railway companies merging to form a range of medium-sized concerns, each with its own territory and ways of doing things. An example is the London & South Western Railway, which had lines from its London terminus at Waterloo to Southampton, Bournemouth and on to the West, eventually reaching Padstow and serving much of North Cornwall.

By World War 1 there existed about 120 railway companies, many of which competed for trade within the same geographical area. However, at the outbreak of war the Government placed all these companies under the central control of the Railway Executive Committee, which was made up of the top people from 10 of the larger railway companies. The Government felt that a unified approach to railway management would result in a more efficient and effective railway system which would help to ensure victory.

After the war the Government decided that this change had been so effective and the railways were so important to industrial and economic growth that they should continue to operate in a non-competitive structure. The Railway Act 1921 grouped all the original separate railway companies into four large companies – the Southern, the Great Western, the London, Midland & Scottish and the London & North Eastern – which came to be known collectively as the 'Big Four'. Each of these huge concerns had its principal territory and therefore acted as more or less the sole carrier of goods and people within that area.

The Big Four continued as separate entities until World War 2, when, again, they were placed under the control of a central body. After the war they were left effectively bankrupt. The Transport Act of 1947 placed the railways under Government control, and the nationalised rail network – British Railways (BR) – was born. BR was tasked with rebuilding and modernising the

Left: By the late 1950s traffic on many rural branch lines had deteriorated to the extent that they simply were not making money and had little prospect of ever doing so again. This was Moreton-hampstead in 1957: hardly a wagon in sight, and only a single coach in the train, and that probably only part-full. Closure to passengers came in 1959, and complete closure in 1964. *A. Attewell*

rail network after the war effort, a task it addressed in 1955 with a massively expensive Modernisation Plan. This included an end to steam traction in Great Britain, which was finally achieved in 1968.

The Modernisation Plan was not entirely successful, and in the mid- to late 1960s large tracts of less profitable railway lines and duplicate routes were closed following the recommendations of Dr Beeching's infamous report, which became generally referred to as the 'Beeching Axe'.

Thereafter Dr Beeching's railway was left more or less unaltered until the mid-1990s, when it was again privatised. Ownership of Britain's rail infrastructure passed to a private company, Railtrack, which provided a safe rail network over which private companies (known as Train Operating Companies or TOCs) could run trains. In 2002 ownership of Britain's rail infrastructure passed to a new 'not for profit' company, Network Rail, which owns and maintains the railway lines in this country today.

Left: BR blue comes to Gorran – one of the new Bachmann BR Class 108 DMUs heads into the tunnel at the end of Gorran Viaduct.

2 Designing a Model Railway

Right: The end of the engine-shed headshunt at Gorran is presumed to be always damp underfoot and is one of those places that feels quite isolated despite the close proximity of the signalman in his signalbox. With a little thought, a real sense of place can be built into a model railway.

Unlike train sets, model railways have a degree of permanence, the track and the landscape being fixed to purpose-built baseboards. For this reason I strongly recommend that you undertake a degree of planning before commencing construction of your model railway. Not only is it financially wasteful to have to do things twice because they were not thought through in the first place, but it is also very demoralising to have to go back and change things because some elementary planning was overlooked.

On the other hand, model railways need not be planned down to the last detail before construction commences. A large amount of time spent thinking about building a model railway without actually running a single train (which is, after all, what building model railways is all about) does not provide a great deal of excitement or reward for the time and money invested.

What is required at the outset of the process is the right amount of planning, and this chapter will outline the most important issues which must be addressed.

It is, of course, possible to construct a model railway without undertaking very much planning at all. Very enjoyable model railways can be built around one or two simple circuits of track

with a few sidings and loops and some generic buildings added to create a landscape around the railway line. There is nothing wrong with this approach, and my earliest model railways were exactly like this. The first was a double-track affair which measured 9ft by 5ft and was constructed on four baseboards. Unfortunately it prompted remonstrations from the domestic department of the house, and a smaller project was required. The resulting second attempt was mostly single-track and was constructed on a baseboard of about 6ft by 4ft which hinged in the middle and folded in on itself for ease of storage. I derived a huge amount of pleasure from these railways, but they were very generic and not really rooted in any particular time or region. As I grew older I started to want a model railway which indicated more clearly where and when it was modelled.

A sense of time and place

The location and era of a model railway are important choices, and they will have a substantial impact upon the appearance of the final model. The choice of stock run, road vehicles modelled and building materials used will be heavily influenced by the period of the layout. Similarly, the shape of the landscape and style of buildings and structures, both inside and outside the railway company fence, will be affected by the region in which the model is based.

The choice of region and era will probably already have been made subconsciously before even the decision to build a model railway in the first place has been consciously taken. We all know which particular railway companies, lines and eras interest us the most amongst the huge variety that has existed on Britain's railway network. However, it is important at the outset to stop and think about the direction in which a particular model railway is heading and to define it reasonably accurately. Questions that crop up during the construction of the rest of the layout can then easily be answered. For example, when you find yourself wondering what type of road vehicle is appropriate for the station yard, you can soon find an answer if you know to within a few years the period in which your model railway is set. If choices such as these are made and carefully adhered to, a real sense of time and place will be created, and as a result your layout will look far more realistic.

The type of railway line that is going to form the subject of the model railway must be considered at an early stage. Will the model be a single-track branch line, a double-track main line or a even quadruple-track main line (if you are lucky enough to have a very large railway room)? Will the layout be based around circuits of track, a terminus station at the end of a line or a through station along the length of a railway line? Will it be a junction with another line, simply a stretch of running line or a more unusual location, such as an engine shed?

Again, it is likely that model-railway builders will have a fairly clear idea of what they are likely to construct before they start making conscious choices about the type of railway line they will aim to replicate. We are, after all, generally aware whether we prefer shunting a mixed goods train in the small but challenging goods yard of a wayside country station or sitting back and watching long main-line trains passing each other at speed. However, giving these questions some conscious thought at the outset is important to ensure that the railway has a firm direction before construction begins.

A home for a model railway

Another important factor which will dramatically affect the design of a model railway is where it will spend its life. Will it be stored away when not in use and be put up only when being worked upon or when the trains are running?

Or are you lucky enough to have a room where the layout can be housed permanently?

If the railway is to be set up permanently, which is preferable if at all possible, a home will need to be found for it.

The loft is a fairly traditional place for a model railway to be constructed, but it is a far-from-ideal location, as the average loft is freezing cold in the winter, baking hot in the summer and fairly damp in between. These conditions are desirable neither for the model railway nor for its operators, and the loft should be viewed only as a last resort. The same is true of the majority of garden sheds. Unless they are well built (*i.e.* of brick walled construction with insulated cavity walls, a suspended floor and roof insulation) they are not very secure and not very hospitable for delicate model-railway locomotives or their operators.

A garage attached to the house is a better location, especially if some building work is undertaken to construct a brick or block wall behind the garage door to add security and cut

Below: 'Casterbridge'. An 'OO'-gauge model railway constructed around the walls of a garage, with a lifting bridge across the side door for easy access to the centre of the garage.

out draughts. Laying some carpet on the floor can make an otherwise cold room feel much cosier and softens the floor when you are down on your hands and knees tracing a wiring fault under the layout. The ideal location is, of course, a spare room within the house, although this is an option open only to a lucky minority.

It is certainly preferable to find a location where a model railway can be set up and left *in situ* between train-running sessions or bouts of construction. However, for many of us this is simply impractical, and the layout will need to be dismantled and stored away when not in use. In such cases it is necessary to consider how much storage space is available, for this will have a pronounced influence on the size and depth of the baseboards you will be able to use, as well as on the shape of the scenery. It will also determine whether such features as buildings, trees and signals are fixed to the railway and stored with it or made removable and stored separately. Ideally the model should also be stored in a warm, damp-free environment to prevent warping of timber or cardboard, and the comments made above with regard to permanent homes for layouts apply also to storage areas.

It is important to consider the fact that the supporting legs for the layout will themselves require storage, as these can take up a surprising amount of space. It is also important to make sure that there really is space in your house for the safe storage of model buildings, if these are not to remain on the layout itself. If a small bedroom is allotted to railway modelling, do you want to use all of the available wall space for hanging railway boards, or to include space for a small workbench? A permanently erected workbench makes modelling much easier, as projects can be left part-finished with the paint drying, and tools left to hand between jobs. However, this, unfortunately, is something else that is often impractical within the confines of a family home.

Scales and gauges

Model railways are all a scaled-down version of the real thing, and there are a number of different scales in common use. The most widespread is 4mm:1ft, this being the scale used for the majority of the ready-to-run rolling stock that is available.

The gauge of railway track is defined as the distance between the inside faces of the rails. English standard gauge (which was exported all over the world) is 4ft 8½in, or 1,435mm. The gauge of the model railway track is different for trains of each different scale. For 7mm:ft,

for example, the usual gauge is 32mm, known as 'O' gauge.

There are other common scale and gauge combinations, some of which are listed in the table below. 'OO' gauge is the most commonly used and uses trains built to a scale of 4mm:ft and running on rails 16.5mm apart.

Description	Gauge (mm)	Scale (mm:ft)
'Z' gauge	6.5	1.5
'N' gauge	9	2.062
'OO' gauge	16.5	4
'O' gauge	32	7
Gauge 1	45	10

For narrow-gauge railways there exists a range of scale and gauge combinations with even more unusual-sounding and seemingly arbitrary names. The easiest way to understand what scale is best for you is to go to the local model shop and have a look at the size of the track and trains for all the different scale and gauge combinations.

Description	Gauge (mm)	Scale (mm:ft)
'009' gauge	9	4
'H0m' gauge	12	3.5
'0-16.5' gauge	16.5	7
'SM32' gauge	32	16
'G-45' gauge	45	(variable)

When it comes to choosing a gauge for your model railway there are really two approaches. If you are graduating from a train set to a model railway you may already have a certain amount

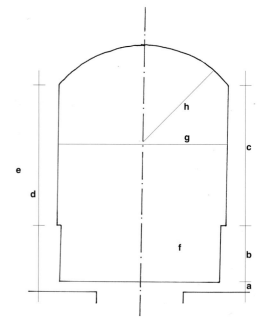

Right: The space required in the vertical plane for trains to pass through bridges and platforms at various common standard-gauge scales. This is usually referred to as the loading-gauge and should be considered when building structures for a model railway. There was a slight variation between the loading-gauges used by the railway companies of the UK; for example the GWR used a generally larger gauge. The figures in the table overleaf are average dimensions.

of track, buildings and rolling stock that you intend to use on your new model railway, so the choice of gauge will already have been made for you. However, if you are starting from scratch, the choice of gauge and scale is often a case of choosing the biggest scale possible which will allow you to fit the layout you wish to build into the room you have available. Bigger scales are much easier to model in and the trains usually run better as they have more weight to keep them on the track, but there are other considerations which come into play. Cost can be a major factor, and larger scale and gauge combinations tend to be more expensive. The availability of ready-made parts and pre-formed track may also be an important consideration, and the number of ready-made parts for 'OO'-gauge model railways still far outstrips that available in other scales.

The distances are marked on the loading-gauge plan right. It is worth checking a train in your chosen scale to ensure that the model is indeed a scale version of the prototype before building a bridge or tunnel to fit it through!

Whatever scale and gauge combination is chosen, this is definitely one decision which must be made before planning of a model railway progresses very far.

The track plan

Determining the track layout and the arrangement of the landscape and structures around the track is one of the most significant pieces of careful planning required during the early stages of layout design.

Dimension	Actual size	Scale dimensions			
		'N' gauge	'OO' gauge'	'O' gauge	Gauge 1
a	6in	1mm	2mm	4mm	5mm
b	3ft	6mm	12mm	21mm	30mm
c	7ft 6in	15mm	30mm	53mm	75mm
d	10ft 9in	22mm	43mm	75mm	108mm
e	12ft 10in	26mm	51mm	90mm	128mm
f	8ft 6in	17mm	34mm	60mm	85mm
g	9ft	18mm	36mm	63mm	90mm
h	5ft 9in	12mm	23mm	40mm	58mm

The enjoyment you derive from operating your model railway will be severely compromised if the track plan makes it awkward to move trains around the layout and lacks interesting challenges, such as well-thought-out goods yards in which to shunt wagons. The credibility of the model will also be undermined if the track plan does not follow the simple rules that were used to design real railways throughout the country, even in the early days, when they were being constructed by a large number of independent companies.

The track plan for a model railway will, of course, be substantially driven by the sort of layout you have decided to build. The alternatives are fairly self-explanatory. It could be a branch line with a single track and a few turnouts, or a main line with two, three, four or even more main running lines and lots of turnouts, crossings and slip crossings. It could be based around a circle contained on the main scenic boards (perhaps partially within a tunnel) or organised in a more linear fashion.

Left: Gorran was built at 4mm:ft scale with 'OO'-gauge track, mainly due to the amount of stock the author already had at this scale. Some of the locomotives are shown here: a scratch-built Beattie well tank can be seen on the left, an old Hornby Dublo Standard Class 4 tank is half-hiding behind the water tower, and a modern model of a GWR pannier tank stands in the locomotive siding.

It is important that the type of layout that can realistically fit into the space available is considered. If an average 4ft-long model railway baseboard was scaled up and marked out on the ground it would actually be fairly small. In 4mm:ft ('OO') scale it would be about 100yd long, which is just about long enough for three scale-length turnouts laid end to end.

Clearly, scale-length turnouts and layouts are actually very long, and some form of compromise over length is generally required. However, this should not be taken too far. Economical use of space is the key, rather than simply cramming as much railway line as possible on a baseboard.

In 4mm:ft scale a single-track country station can be comfortably fitted in a space 8-10ft long and 2ft 6in wide without excessive condensing or cramming. A prototypical double-track station, which is likely to have been more generously laid out in the first place, can usually be fitted in a space around 12-14ft long without feeling overly condensed.

In planning the layout of the track for a particular model railway I find it easiest to start with a simple line diagram showing the major elements, such as branch lines, locomotive sheds, goods yards, platforms and so forth. The detail can then be added around this. If you have more than one running line then each one should be used for a particular direction of travel, rather like the lanes on a road. In double-track situations one line would be termed by railwaymen as the 'up' line, the other the 'down' line. Trains usually travelled 'up' to London, although some railways were different; the Midland Railway, for example, used to travel 'up' to Derby.

Above: The approach to Aberaeron station in the early 1960s. This gently curving layout is typical of the approach to many country stations, but when planning a model of such a location there is a temptation to use the shortest turnouts and fit the layout into the smallest length possible to allow more track to be fitted in elsewhere. This would result in much of the character being lost and an unrealistic-looking model railway. It is much better to be light handed when condensing layouts. Some of the length could be taken out of the line to the engine shed, for example, but some should be left to allow a locomotive to stand outside the shed and to retain the open feeling of the prototype. *A. Attewell*

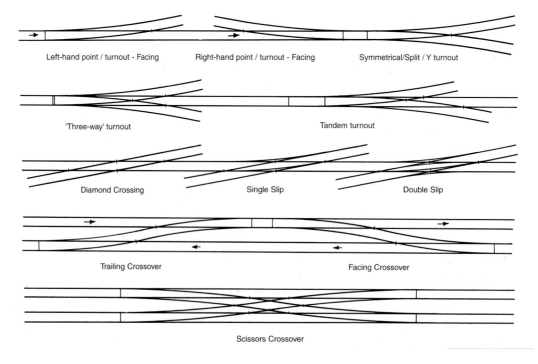

Basic Point Formations

Left-hand point / turnout - Facing   Right-hand point / turnout - Facing   Symmetrical/Split / Y turnout

'Three-way' turnout   Tandem turnout

Diamond Crossing   Single Slip   Double Slip

Trailing Crossover   Facing Crossover

Scissors Crossover

Right: Some of the most common elements of railway track layouts. These can be used to develop a track plan for a model railway, which can then be converted into an order for track.

Left: Real railway trackwork at Par, Cornwall. On the right of the picture can be seen a pair of double slips, providing access to the goods sidings from the Newquay-line platform. Double slips can be a valuable space-saving piece of trackwork, as they effectively comprise of two back-to-back turnouts but take up much less space. *A. Attewell*

Left: Examining aerial photographs is a good way to gain inspiration when planning a model railway. This is Moorswater, just outside Liskeard, Cornwall, in 1957. The old Liskeard & Caradon Railway locomotive shed seen in so many railway paintings is visible towards the top of the photograph, together with a typical industrial layout of sidings and a short loop. Also of interest are the houses surrounding the railway and the extent of the valley sides that has been turned into vegetable gardens. This photograph is not actually an aerial view but was taken from the adjacent main-line viaduct. A photograph taken in the opposite direction can be found in Chapter 8. *A. Attewell*

Where there are three, four or more tracks, these are often grouped by speed. There would almost always be two main tracks, which would usually be known as the up and down fast or main. Additional tracks, such as the up local, down slow, up goods, down relief (a Western Region term) and so forth were added as required. Sidings were also often named so that they could easily be distinguished, for example the 'Baltic Siding' at Winchester, Hampshire, which was constructed to send troops and supplies to the Baltic.

In order to move trains from one parallel track to another the railways would use two turnouts joined together and operated at the same time – a crossover. Both turnouts would always either be set for their straight-through routes or for a train to cross over from one track to the other. An example is situated on the viaduct at Gorran to allow trains leaving the goods loop or the goods yard in the up direction to cross back onto the up main line.

As each running line generally has a specific direction of travel, all the turnouts along its length will generally be approached in a particular direction. If the train usually travels from the 'toe' of the turnout (where the switches are) and travels towards the 'crossing' then the turnout is termed a facing turnout or facing point. If, on the other hand, a train travelling in its normal direction of travel arrives at the end of the turnout containing the crossing and travels towards the turnouts, it is termed a trailing point. These trailing switches are less prone to sending a train in the wrong direction by mistake (which could cause it to crash into another train) because they do not make an actual decision about which way the train will go.

Right: The approaches to Hardwick Central, the main terminus station of Ian Allan's 7¼ in-gauge Great Cockcrow Railway, which is located near Chertsey, just off the M25. The track layout at this station has been extremely well thought out, and an afternoon spent watching the trains here and understanding how the layout operates would be time well invested for anyone planning a major terminus.

Wherever possible (in some cases with an almost incredible single-mindedness) railways would avoid facing points and use trailing points, and model layouts should reflect this. An example of this rule in action can be seen in the orientation of the turnout giving access to the locomotive yard at Gorran. A facing point on the up line would be the obvious solution, giving direct access to the engine shed, but it would be unlikely that a facing point would have been used here. Locomotives on their own are quite manoeuvrable and would simply have been expected to reverse twice.

Facing and trailing crossovers can easily be identified, as the two turnouts involved will be orientated in the same direction relative to the direction of traffic on both lines. Both crossovers on the portion of Gorran that has been constructed so far are trailing. The only facing point on a running line (the distinction is much less important on non-passenger-carrying lines) is that into the goods yard.

Crossovers are also often used at the exit of goods yards and sidings to provide a measure of protection against a wagon overcoming its brakes and rolling out of the sidings onto the main line. Just such an arrangement is installed at Gorran at the exit to the goods yard. The turnout off the main line into the goods yard, and the turnout out of the goods yard into the feed store work together so that, if the turnout into the yard is set for the main line, the turnout on the way out of the yard is set to divert any runaway wagons into the feed store. It therefore acts as protection for the down main line, as it would direct a wagon rolling out of the goods yard away from the passenger-carrying track.

Right: The track layout of Gorran laid out on the engine-shed baseboard. The up and down lines are easily recognisable in the centre, on foam underlay. The up line is on the right, and trains travel from the top to the bottom of the picture. The down line is on the left, with trains travelling up the page. The goods loop and yard are clearly connected via a facing connection onto the down main line, whereas the locomotive shed and yard trails onto the up main.

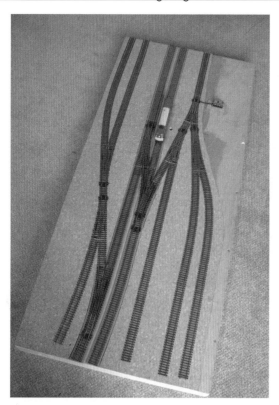

Trap points (short points with switches but without a crossing) are also used to achieve the same result, often where a crossover would serve no useful purpose.

A loop is the name given to a parallel track laid next to a single line which connects to the single line with a turnout at either end. They are rather like laybys on roads and allow the locomotive to 'run round' its train from one end to the other. The same function can be performed by means of two crossovers between double-track main lines. Such an arrangement exists at Gorran, one trailing crossover being situated on the viaduct and one situated in front of the signalbox, both connecting the up and down main lines.

For readers who are not sure where to start with a track plan, or who are seeking some inspiration, I have included over the following pages a number of track layouts which I believe would all make very enjoyable and prototypical model railways.

Left: Part of Gorran laid out on the lounge floor, with various possible sizes of baseboard marked out in masking tape and a few part-complete buildings placed in their eventual locations. This is a useful process, as things like different turnout radii can be tried and the most appropriate selected. The water tower was later moved to improve the visual balance of the layout and avoid a conglomeration of buildings at either end of the baseboard with nothing in the middle. Paper turnout templates are being used where the track has yet to be purchased. These can be obtained from Peco for the price of a few stamps and are very useful at this stage.

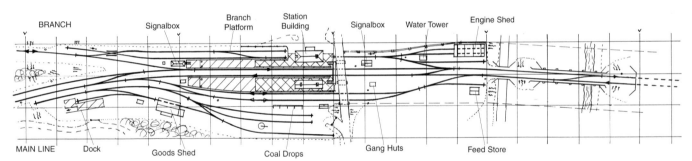

BRANCH   Signalbox   Branch Platform   Station Building   Signalbox   Water Tower   Engine Shed

MAIN LINE   Dock   Goods Shed   Coal Drops   Gang Huts   Feed Store

Above: The track layout for the whole of Gorran. Once this had been established the landscape was designed and added around the railway to create the plan for the complete model.

Left: The station at Helston, Cornwall, in 1957. Helston was a very compact branch-line terminus including all of the most common railway buildings. The locomotive shed and water tower are to the right of this view, the signalbox and station building being just discernible at the centre, and the goods shed at the rear of the station.
A. Attewell

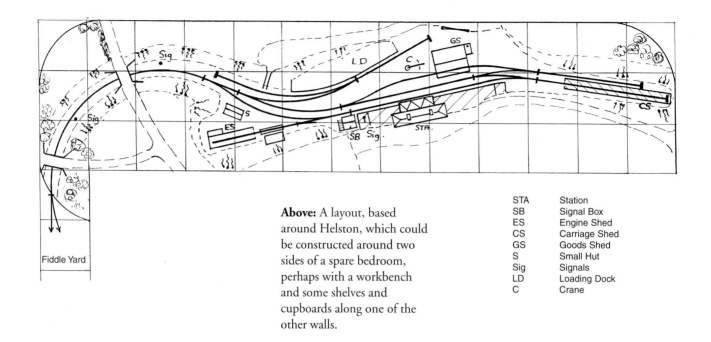

Fiddle Yard

Above: A layout, based around Helston, which could be constructed around two sides of a spare bedroom, perhaps with a workbench and some shelves and cupboards along one of the other walls.

STA	Station
SB	Signal Box
ES	Engine Shed
CS	Carriage Shed
GS	Goods Shed
S	Small Hut
Sig	Signals
LD	Loading Dock
C	Crane

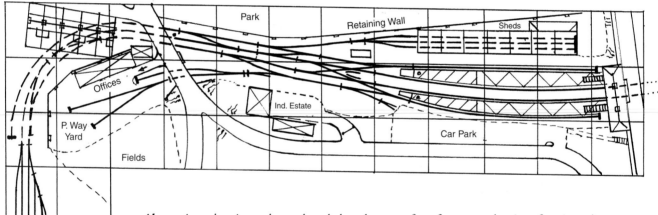

Above: A modern image layout loosely based on the Metropolitan Railway platforms at Baker Street. Again, this model railway could be arranged around two sides of a room. The lines between the platforms could continue, as here, if space is available or the layout could be changed into a terminus. A shed has been added for train storage and an engineers' yard is included on the left-hand side, which would add some interesting shunting to the layout and would provide a reason

for a few unusual trains of engineers' wagons to make an appearance in between electric or diesel trains running into the platforms. The turnout almost entering the car park is purely aesthetic, but is typical of many stations where goods yards have been quickly taken up and converted into car parks or industrial estates. The unprototypically sharp curves required to access the storage sidings are hidden within the tunnel — a useful trick.

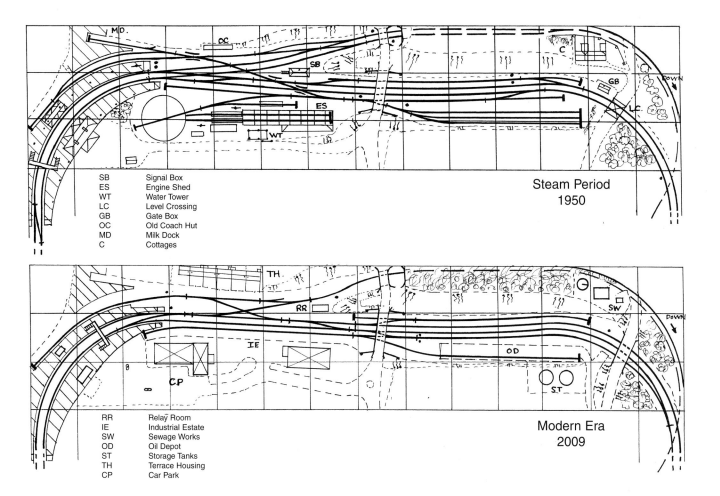

SB	Signal Box
ES	Engine Shed
WT	Water Tower
LC	Level Crossing
GB	Gate Box
OC	Old Coach Hut
MD	Milk Dock
C	Cottages

Steam Period
1950

RR	Relay Room
IE	Industrial Estate
SW	Sewage Works
OD	Oil Depot
ST	Storage Tanks
TH	Terrace Housing
CP	Car Park

Modern Era
2009

Above: An interesting variation on a theme demonstrating how the style of track layouts has changed over time. Throughout the BR period, the use of diamonds and slips has been much reduced due to the fact that they require more maintenance than plain turnouts. There is also less demand for such flexible layouts now that less freight is shunted around individual stations, which is demonstrated here by a significant reduction in the number of sidings provided at this hypothetical station. One of these layouts (or perhaps even both) could be constructed around the walls of a garage.

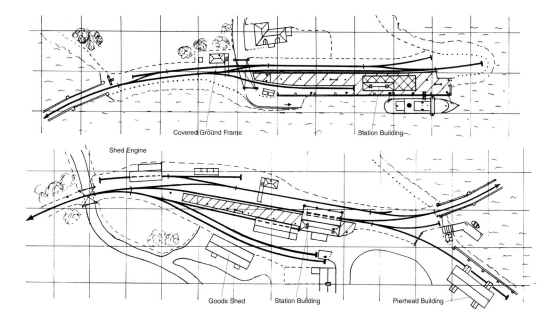

Covered Ground Frame

Station Building

Shed Engine

Goods Shed   Station Building   Pierhead Building

Left: Lymington Pier and Lymington Town. These two small stations on a single-track branch line could make fascinating models due to their seaside location. In reality they are only a short distance apart, and, if space permits, both could be arranged around the walls of a small railway room to create an interesting and rewarding little railway system.

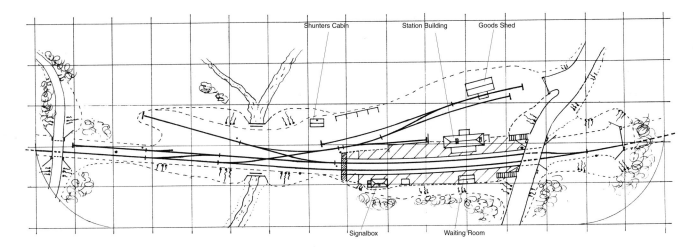

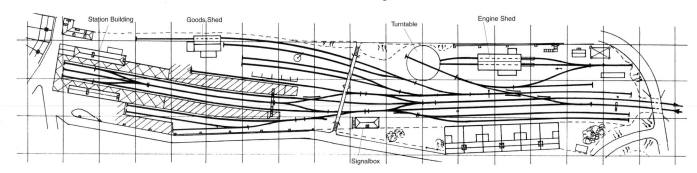

Above: West Meon. This spacious through station on a single-track branch line includes an interesting and unusual track layout in the goods yard, albeit one that was common to the whole Meon Valley line. This could be realistically represented in 'OO' by careful selection of components from the various ranges of track available.

Below: Milton Low Level. A fictitious double-track terminus with a Northern and industrial feel to the track plan. There is plenty of operational potential here, and this could be a very enjoyable model to construct and operate. It could, perhaps, be constructed in a shed or garage with a decent stretch of double-track main line laid out in the garden, perhaps returning to some storage sidings along the other side of the railway room. The location of baseboard joints would need some careful thought before construction commenced!

Storage sidings

It is not essential to include storage sidings on a model railway. My first layout had no dedicated storage sidings, and the whole layout was scenic. However, as I progressed towards more carefully considered representations of railways I started to introduce some storage sidings. These were often located in tunnels or hidden behind retaining walls and were used to store spare locomotives out of view of the main scenic portion of the layout, which kept the occupancy of the locomotive sheds at more believable levels for the size of stations I modelled.

As I moved on towards linear model railways which more accurately represented country railway stations, storage sidings increased in importance.

The easiest way of providing train storage is to split the incoming railway line(s) into a large number of sidings through a 'fan' of pointwork; this arrangement is shown in the plan based on Baker Street, which can be found on page 20. The actual number of sidings required is a personal choice and is dictated by the number of trains you will need to store at any one time. To avoid taking up a large proportion of layout's length with pointwork you should use the shortest radius points that will give trouble-free running. Consideration should also be given to the layout of the pointwork, to make sure that it is as short as possible.

The trouble with the siding approach is that it is difficult to change the trains around and all too easy to trap the locomotive you want at the end of a siding. It is therefore better to provide loops in which to store the trains, so that the ends of all

Left: The storage sidings on Casterbridge. A series of long loops is provided with engine sidings at either end of many of them, some visible on the right. These loops enable easy alteration of trains passing through the storage sidings, as well as storage of items of stock between appearances on the scenic side of the layout.

the sidings are brought back together again into one track. Locomotives can then be released for their next duty, and wagons or coaches more easily changed around between trains.

If loops are laid out beyond the end of the scenic portion the layout will start to become very long. It may be preferable to arrange the storage sidings directly behind it, with either a curve beyond the scenic portion, to turn the trains around and present them to the storage sidings, or a reversing siding to reach those installed behind the layout. If you are modelling a through station one set of loops can be arranged at the rear of the layout, with curves at either end, making it into a big oval.

There are a large number of alternative, more compact ways in which storage sidings can be constructed. A good way of picking up ideas is

to have a look at other people's layouts at railway exhibitions. Most seem to use a subtly different system which works particularly well for each specific model railway. To create storage sidings, some people employ systems involving

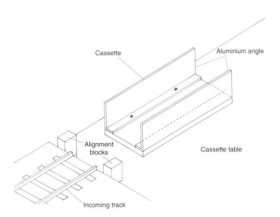

Above: Another variation on the theme of train storage and re-marshalling: this is often referred to as the 'cassette' system. Individual cassettes are made up of a timber base with angle aluminium or similar screwed to the side. The trains run along the edges of the aluminium angles. Lots of cassettes can be lined up on a flat surface and held together with bulldog clips for electrical connectivity. The train can then be run onto the cassette and uncoupled onto different sections of cassette which makes it easy to re-arrange trains or swap locomotives. A system to ensure alignment of the cassette to the incoming track needs to be constructed and ideally provided with a means of supplying and isolating electrical supply to the cassette.

Above: Sliding or rotating tables for the storage of trains. The arrangement shown on the left is often called a traverser, and that on the right a sector plate. If space permits this can be made to rotate through 360°, and trains can thus be turned around in their entirety before being returned to the layout. Good bearings and running strips are essential to both of these systems — some lateral thinking in a DIY store usually provides handy components.

Above: When including storage sidings beyond the scenic portion of a model railway some kind of visual break is desirable between the scenic and non-scenic portions of the layout. Tunnels are frequently (perhaps a little too frequently) used to achieve this, as are bridges or cuttings. A model of a bridge such as this one, at Newcastle Emlyn, in West Wales, would form a perfect visual break to the end of a layout. Some of the foreground interest visible here could also be included to distract the eye from trying to catch a glimpse of the storage sidings under the bridge. The bridge could be constructed hard against the edge of the board or, if space permits, a short section of the cutting beyond the bridge could be included to make the position of the bridge appear a little less contrived. *A. Attewell*

sliding or rotating tables which can dispense altogether with the need for pointwork, freeing up space for the scenic section.

Baseboards and the shape of the landscape

Once a track plan has been established, practicalities like fitting it onto some baseboards need to be considered. The chapter after next discusses the different types of baseboard which can be used as a foundation for a model railway. I recommend that you give this chapter a read before embarking on the design of your baseboards, as there are a number of important issues to be considered.

The easiest way to decide upon the dimensions for your baseboards is to draw your layout out to scale, photocopy the resulting plan and then draw on possible baseboard sizes, ensuring at all costs that the joints between the boards do not pass through pointwork. Once the baseboards have been set out around the track plan the shape of the landscape should be considered. There is a tendency at this stage to design the landscape around the railway, but it is important to remember that, in real life, the landscape will have come first.

Once you feel sufficient design has been undertaken for your layout to avoid the need for major changes later on, it is time to get started on some baseboards. As already mentioned, the process of baseboard construction is dealt with at length in Chapter 4.

Right: A goods train crosses the lane bridge at Gorran. An open-frame baseboard is required to allow features such as this, where the level of the landscape is below that of the line.

24

Left: Woodworking tools. A cup of tea, ideally kept warm and full by the domestic department, is of course essential.

Perhaps the most important tool for railway modelling is a place where modelling can be undertaken. A well-lit space near a window which is also well served by artificial lighting, for modelling during the long winter evenings, is ideal. The space does not have to be permanently allocated to modelling, although this is undoubtedly desirable. A shelf or some cupboard space is also useful for storing small pots of paint, tubes of glue, unbuilt kits and the like.

The other tools frequently required during model railway construction are discussed briefly in this chapter and can be seen in use throughout the rest of the book. None of them is particularly unusual or specialised, and most can be found in the average toolbox.

A modelling surface

A modelling surface protects the table or bench where modelling is undertaken from being damaged with a knife or covered in spilt paint. A piece of wood such as a sheet of chipboard could be used, but I find that a specially designed cutting mat is by far the best option. Such mats are made from a rubber-like material which does not become heavily scored when cut and does not blunt the sharp point of a modelling knife. I recommend purchasing the largest you can afford; the one I use is A2 size.

However, readers should be aware that cutting mats are not suitable for use when soldering, as they are prone to melt. Instead, a rectangle of wood such as hardboard is required for this activity. It is also useful to have a piece of scrap wood available on which to drill, to prevent damage to your cutting mat or soldering board should you drill a little too far.

Woodworking tools

Woodworking tools are required for baseboard construction, which is discussed in Chapter 4. Normal hand tools, which most people will already have for household DIY, are more than adequate.

A good workmate is a very worthwhile investment if you are likely to do a reasonable amount of woodwork as it makes life considerably easier. Beady-eyed readers will notice that there are two workmates in some of the photographs in this book. It is not essential to purchase two workmates to allow you to build a model railway, but, if you can bear the expense, it does make cutting big sheets of plywood and long lengths of strip wood much less awkward. A good sharp saw is a necessity, and a hand-held countersink is a useful tool, as it avoids the need to repeatedly change the bit in your drill. A good battery-powered electric drill is useful when building

Below: The author's favourite Stanley knife is rather battered and has seen some service over the years! Spare Stanley-knife blades can be seen to the right, and a second cheap and, frankly, quite nasty knife is shown at the bottom which is permanently fitted with a blade for cutting grooves in plasticard, rather than cutting through it. The range of files commonly used when modelling include a small flat needle, a round needle, a 4in second-cut and a 6in coarse, used for heavy jobs. A rough-tapered half-round file is also handy.

Far right: Buying the best pliers you can afford is well worth the money invested. Box-jointed pliers and side cutters are best, although even top-quality side cutters go blunt after a while and need replacing every few years. From top to bottom, the tools on the left are flat-nosed pliers, side cutters and round-nosed pliers. The tool to the right is for cutting and stripping electrical wire.

baseboards for drilling holes for screws and wiring, and if you are constructing open-framed baseboards the use of a jigsaw will make profiling parts of the baseboard to follow the contours of the landscape much quicker and easier.

Modelling tools

When it comes to modelling tools the most important is undoubtedly a good knife. I use an old Stanley knife for all purposes and change the blade regularly to make sure it is sharp. A good steel ruler, clearly marked, is also required. A selection of files, such as those shown below, is helpful for tasks such as straightening up edges in plastic kits or adjusting the shape of the end of a cut rail so that it accepts a fishplate.

A good range of drills and drill bits is important for modelling. A standard wheelbrace is useful for drilling larger holes in timber or plasticard by hand power, and a small Archimedes drill is perfect for smaller (below 1mm diameter) drill bits. One of these drills, along with a selection of small drill bits, is shown in use in Chapter 5 during the track-laying process. A pin vice is useful when trying to hold drill bits in the 1-3mm range.

In addition, a selection of good paintbrushes is required. As a minimum, good-quality brushes, ideally with squirrel or sable bristles, of sizes 000, 0 and 2, should be purchased. They should be thoroughly washed in thinners after every use and treated with care. Some rough brushes for landscape work are also useful, and some bigger (1in) brushes can be used for painting large areas with glue for sticking down cork underlay and similar tasks.

A range of screwdrivers is, of course, required. Small electrical screwdrivers find uses for the usual wiring jobs or for taking model locomotives apart. A set of small cross-head (Philips) screwdrivers, as sold for jewellery work,

can also be useful. Wire strippers are needed for wiring and fine-nosed pliers and side cutters can be helpful in many modelling situations.

If soldering is going to be undertaken, a small 15W soldering-iron or similar is ideal for the majority of tasks. Some solder and flux will also be required, as will a soldering-iron stand.

The above does not constitute an exhaustive list of tools required but includes those that are likely be used repeatedly. In my opinion it is always worth buying the best that you can afford, as expensive tools are generally quality items that will serve you longer and better than their cheaper counterparts.

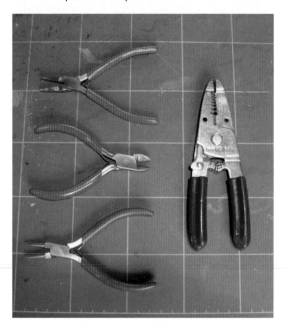

Below: Soldering tackle. Pictured is a pen-type applicator for the liquid flux used by the author; such items can be picked up at exhibitions. A paintbrush will do a very similar job. If a paste-type flux is used, a cocktail stick or a match can be employed to move a tiny piece of flux to wherever it is required.

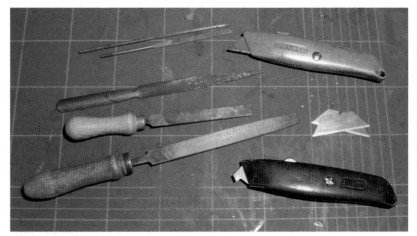

Baseboard Construction 4

Left: The main scenic boards for Yes Tor Junction slope from front to back to provide depth to the landscape without making the individual boards excessively deep. This is certainly an option when modelling the foothills of Dartmoor (as was the case here), but it does make baseboard construction a significant three-dimensional challenge!

Train sets are transient affairs, set up in one configuration one day and a different one the next, with perhaps a few out-of-the box model buildings dotted here and there to add a representation of the landscape beyond the company fence. Model railways are different. They are a recreation of a railway landscape, with careful thought paid to the layout of the track, the surrounding buildings and the landscape in which they are set, and can take years to perfect.

To begin the transition from train set to model railway you will first need to construct baseboards. These will form a permanent home for your model railway; the solid base to which everything else will be fixed. They will allow the easy transportation of a 400ft-long main-line station by breaking it down into small discrete sections and, with a bit of thought, they will afford it protection while it is being stored. They will shape the landscape through which the trains will travel and the supporting legs will elevate the iron road to a comfortable viewing height, meaning you can forget the knee pain associated with a day playing with your train set on the carpet forever!

If you are lucky enough to have space in your house for a railway to be erected permanently within its own 'railway room', and you have no aspiration to take it to an exhibition, then you will be able to ignore many of the finer points of this chapter. There will, for example, be no need to agonise over the location of baseboard joints, as you will be able to simply build one continuous baseboard along the lines explained here and lay the track without having to adjust it around your chosen unit of baseboard length. For the majority of us, however, our model railway will need breaking down and storing, and this chapter explains how this can best be achieved.

Design

The design of the baseboards merits careful consideration. As previously discussed, it is worth thinking about how the railway will fit onto its baseboards during the early stages of design, making sure that there are gaps in pointwork, at regularly spaced intervals, which can be used for baseboard joints. However, do not let the baseboard layout overly dictate the design of your model railway. At the outset, greater emphasis should be placed on getting a track layout which you are happy with and a pleasing design to the scenery surrounding the railway. Minor tweaks at a later date can usually ensure that it fits onto the baseboards.

Right: A view inside the storage unit formed from a pair of boards for Yes Tor Junction. This demonstrates how tightly one section of landscape can be made to fit into another. This is a 7mm-scale model, and consequently the bridges, buildings and trees are quite large. These have been made removable to reduce the size of the storage unit.

Below: Flat-topped baseboard country: Kingsbridge, Devon, 1957. The bulk of the area inside the company fence is completely flat with the exception of the cutting side (to the right of this photograph), which could easily be added to the edge of a flat-topped board using polystyrene as a landscape-former. *A. Attewell*

It is usually best to try to build all the baseboards for a layout to the same dimensions. This is not an absolute rule and it is one I frequently break, but it undoubtedly makes board storage and transportation significantly easier.

As a general rule, baseboards which are approximately 2ft x 4ft (600mm x 1,200mm) in size are easy to handle and a sensible weight once complete. It is perfectly possible to construct a layout with a longitudinal split down the middle with pairs of baseboards joining along their long edge; however, this often results in track crossing the joint between baseboards at a very shallow angle. I counsel you against planning tracks to cross the edge of baseboards at anything less than a 60° angle between the rail and the baseboard joint. It is very difficult to lay the track across this kind of joint and poor running is likely to be encountered as the breaks in each rail will not be opposite each other.

A useful by-product of building solid baseboards is that they can be used to provide protection to the railway when it is being stored. Simple plywood end plates can be bolted to a pair of baseboards of the same dimensions with the scenic faces turned inwards, providing a robust box-like structure. This has the added advantage of protecting the ends of the rails at baseboard joints, which can otherwise be vulnerable to damage, behind a sheet of plywood. If employing this technique, consideration should be given at the design stage to the profile of the landscape of the two boards which are to be paired, to avoid the final two-board unit becoming too deep.

There are two main categories of baseboard: those with a complete flat top and those without. A flat-topped baseboard is the simplest to construct and is really just a table built to the dimensions and height required, on which the model railway can be constructed. Flat-topped baseboards are often most appropriate for a station area, where there are a large number of lines at the same level.

The alternative is an open-frame baseboard. This is often more appropriate for the ends of a layout, where the railway is frequently modelled travelling through the landscape. The track is laid on a trackbase which is cut to the required dimensions and fixed onto the baseboard, but the rest of the baseboard is left open. Cross-members are cut to provide a framework for the landscape around the railway.

The rest of this chapter discusses construction of these two different types of baseboard individually. Hybrids of the two are, of course, possible.

Flat-topped baseboards

Flat-topped baseboards are essentially tables on which a model railway can be constructed. They are by far the simplest to construct, and no specialist carpentry skills are required. They are particularly well suited to models of stations, where there are wide areas of flat ground.

Baseboards for model railways are generally made of timber. They could in theory be fabricated from steel (or these days probably in plastic), but wood is a material with which we are all familiar, is relatively inexpensive and is easy to work using basic tools.

Above: Batch production is a much more efficient way of producing items like these little blocks than cutting each one out when it is required. In this photograph the ends of the blocks are being sanded. Just one firm drag across the sheet for each edge of each end is usually all that is required to neaten it.

I often use plywood for the flat surface of my railway boards. It is readily available and relatively cheap and easy to work, but it can be quite difficult to get track pins into the hard surface of the wood. A better (albeit slightly more expensive) material is Sundeala board, which is a man-made board created from densely compressed newsprint, meaning track pins can be easily knocked or often even pushed into

place allowing easy adjustment until the track layout is just right.

Sundeala board is slightly more difficult to obtain than plywood, the best source these days being specialist firms advertising in the model-railway press. Due to the fact that Sundeala board is less strong than plywood it should be stored flat if possible (it can curl up under its weight if stored on its end) and needs supporting with a baseboard cross brace every 250mm or so — a closer spacing than that needed for plywood. Despite these drawbacks I would recommend Sundeala for trackbases, as it is so much easier to get the track pins into the baseboard. However, if Sundeala is not for you, plywood will do the job, as it did for me with Gorran.

MDF would dictate the use of rather solid track pins which would look quite unsightly in smaller scales. The dust produced when cutting and working MDF can also upset the respiratory system, meaning a mask should be used at all times when working with the material, which would become quite tiresome when constructing a large number of baseboards.

I use large quantities of softwood. This is sold in various sizes and is useful for the framework for the baseboard, for the legs and for the little blocks which seem to be needed in their thousands to form screwed connections. It is worth shopping around when buying this timber as some DIY stores sell much better quality wood than others. Timber which is straight when bought

Bottom left: Drilling a stack of cross-members with a pillar drill to ensure that all the holes will line up for the point-operating cords. It is, of course, important to ensure that the cross-members are all installed the same way round after drilling. If a large number of cross-members causes the stack to become unmanageably high, one member can be drilled and used as a template for the rest. This is also a useful technique when drilling the holes with a hand drill and reduces the number of hands required to something closer to the number available!

Bottom right:
The parts required to construct a flat-topped baseboard. This example is 4ft 10in long x 1ft 10in wide. The flat top is evident, as are the long side members (to the right) and the ends and cross-members (left), complete with holes for wiring and point-operating cords. The smaller pieces of wood in the centre include blocks and keeper plates (at the bottom) for constructing the sockets for the legs. The larger square blocks (with two holes drilled across the diagonal) will be screwed inside the end of the side members to add extra thickness to this area. These blocks will form one side of the leg socket. The smaller blocks will form the other side, and the keeper plates the rear.

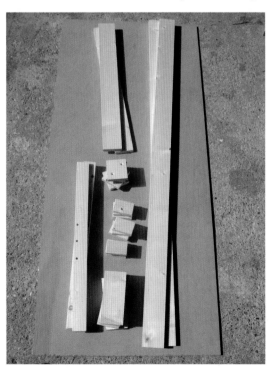

Right: A completed leg socket with a leg installed. The location of the various blocks can be clearly seen. The keeper plate is held in place with the two screws, which can also be used to adjust the tightness of the leg within the socket. They should not be too tight, or it can be very difficult to insert the leg into the hole.

and which has the fewest knots possible is very much easier to work with, and it is well worth paying a little more to ensure good-quality wood.

When I embark upon the task of constructing a baseboard my first job is to produce a dozen or so blocks of timber measuring 2in x 1in (or the nearest metric equivalent). These should be as long as the side-members forming the framework of the baseboard are deep and will come in very handy, as will become apparent. I usually use a mitre block, to make sure the ends are square, and then clean any potential splinters off the ends by running each edge across a sheet of sandpaper.

Once the required number of blocks, plus a few spare, has been cut out the next step is to cut out the long members that will run along the front and the rear of the baseboard and the baseboard ends. It is easiest to fashion these from 3in x 1in strip wood, although a lightweight beam section can be made up from 2in x 1in blocks and 6mm ply if preferred. This system is well described in the book *Landscape Modelling* by Barry Norman, details of which can be found in the 'Recommended Reading' list.

Cutting out the cross-members to help support the centre of the baseboard is the next step. Again, 2in x 1in timber is ideal, and they should be spaced every foot or so. It is a good idea to drill a few holes through the cross-members to allow wiring and any nylon cord (used to operate turnouts and signals) to pass along the layout. Ideally, these holes should line up through each cross-member. If you have access to a pillar drill, this can be used to drill holes through all the cross-members at the same time. A similar result can be achieved by using a hand-held electric drill, drilling onto a block of scrap wood to protect the drill bit, but you do need about five hands to hold everything in place!

Right: The underside of the completed baseboard, showing how everything fits together. This represents about an afternoon's hard work.

Open-frame baseboards

There is no complete flat top on an open frame baseboard. Instead, a trackbase is cut to the width required, and cross-members take on an additional role as landscape-formers.

Open-frame baseboards are constructed in a similar manner to the flat-topped baseboards described above. The sides are again cut from 3in x 1in timber, and end plates added to form the basic frame of the board. The end plates should be made from plywood (rather than the stripwood used previously), and this should be cut to follow the shape of the land.

Cutting out the trackbase requires slightly more thought when constructing an open-frame

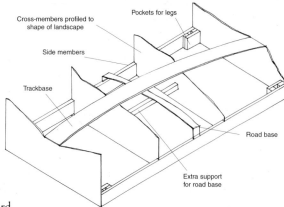

Cross-members profiled to shape of landscape

Pockets for legs

Side members

Trackbase

Road base

Extra support for road base

Right: A simple open-framed baseboard.

baseboard. The trackbase is likely to extend only an inch or so either side of the track, or slightly further if buildings are to be included beside the line.

Great care should be taken at this stage to ensure that the trackbase is cut to the dimensions required. It is easy to rush the process of setting out the track in a spurt of eagerness to get the board together, which may result in an awkward kink in the final track layout. It is best to spend some time physically laying out the track on the plywood, perhaps using paper point templates as shown in Chapter 3. Once you are happy with the layout, mark the edge of the trackbase required on the plywood with a pencil, remembering to leave enough width on either side of the track for the ballast and, alongside, a walkway ('cess' in railway parlance), which in reality is usually about 3ft wide.

Once the trackbase has been constructed the cross-members can be cut out to fit around it and hold the baseboard together. It is also easiest to make these cross-members from plywood rather than the strip wood used for flat-topped baseboards. I usually use more cross-members for an open-frame baseboard than a flat-topped board, spacing them at about 9in centres. If the gap between the members is too great, the cardboard and *papier mâché* landscape tends to sag between them. I find it easiest initially to cut rectangular cross-members of the correct width and maximum height required from a sheet of plywood with a normal handsaw before later profiling the top with a jigsaw.

It is important to ensure that the slopes introduced to a model railway's landscape are realistic and, if the railway is representative of a particular area, that they are authentic. The natural topography of this country ranges from the essentially flat lands of East Anglia to the mountains of Snowdonia and Cumbria, and this should be reflected on model railways set in these areas. The reason for these differences lies in the geology, and this can have a pronounced effect on the slope of a railway cutting or embankment which has been engineered

Below: A behind-the-scenes view of Gorran, showing some of the cross-members and some lengths of stripwood in use to support the roadbase at the required elevation.

Below: Contrasting
terrain in rural
Cornwall: rolling hills
frame a china-clay train
on the line to Fowey.
This photograph was
actually taken from the
guard's van rather from
underneath a bridge as
might at first appear to
be the case. *A. Attewell*

through the landscape. Cuttings through rock can sometimes be so steep-sided that the walls are almost vertical, whereas cuttings through sandy soil usually have much more gently sloping sides, as sand will not long stand up at a steep angle. Clay is a much better material for cutting construction and is probably the type of soil through which the majority of railways in this country have been constructed.

The slope of cuttings and embankments can often be exaggerated on a model railway so that it remains in proportion to other distances, which have also been compressed. Slopes of about 2:1 should be used for sandy areas, whereas around 1:1 can be used to represent cuttings through clay. Rock cuttings should never be completely vertical, but they can be fairly close.

If a gentle rise is required in the landscape, a good way to ensure that the slope or shape of the land does not change too dramatically between one cross-member and the next is to use each previous cross-member as a template while marking the subsequent one. Keeping the pencil a more or less constant distance from the edge already cut will prevent any sudden changes in angle of the finished hillside.

Once the cross-members have been cut out and drilled with any holes necessary for wiring or point-operating mechanisms they can be fixed between the side-members of the board using the universal 2in x 1in blocks. The trackbase can then be added, the joint between it and the cross-member being made using yet more 2in x 1in stripwood. The length of this should be cut to match the width of the trackbase. If these lengths of stripwood are screwed to the trackbase first, any slight adjustment required to keep the trackbase level and flat can be made before screwing the joining piece to the cross-member, locking the trackbase in the correct position.

Once the trackbase has been positioned on the baseboard any further supporting woodwork required can be constructed. This often includes bases for buildings which are not at track level

Above: An open-topped baseboard in the course of construction, demonstrating the different levels that can be incorporated. The trackbase can be seen in the centre of the board on the right, elevated in this case above the surface of the board. The base for the viaduct to sit on can be seen at a lower level on the left, and two cross-members/landscape-formers are visible in the foreground. The one on the right has been cut out as a blank square and still requires profiling, while that on the left has been cut around the trackbase and has been profiled. Notches have also been cut into the ends of this cross-member to carry it over the side members of the baseboard.

and, therefore, have not been included in the trackbase and any bases required for roads. I usually add these in 6mm plywood, sometimes gluing them between cross-members with a glue gun rather than adding yet more blocks to the baseboard for screwed connections. This keeps down the weight of the baseboard and is easily strong enough for the purpose. Once this process has been completed the baseboard is ready for the landscape surface and, much more importantly, some trains!

Supporting legs

The simplest way of constructing supporting legs for a baseboard is to use lengths of 2in x 1in timber cut to the appropriate length and inserted into the corner of each board. Only one board on the layout needs to be self-supporting on its own four feet. The rest can be bolted to the previous board at one end 'piggy-backed' off the first board and supported by a pair of legs at the other end. Once they are set up, these two-legged and two-bolted boards are quite firm enough for their purpose.

If legs of 2in x 1in timber are used they can be attached to the baseboard by locating in the

Above right: The supporting structure for the lane at the end of the yard at Gorran. The start of the piece of timber which supports the viaduct can be discerned on the right.

Below: A single-leg support for a narrow baseboard. Timber 2in square is ideal for the upright, while the diagonal braces are best fabricated out of steel strip. If bolted connections are used throughout, the leg can fold up to reduce required storage space.

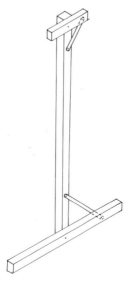

Above: Under-baseboard strutting for a wider baseboard. Clear identification of all struts by type is essential. The author uses A, B, C etc to match particular legs to corresponding sockets on the baseboard, because it is important that the correct leg goes in the coorect hole to ensure that the bolts are in the right place for the bracing. Careful setting-out of the bolts for the struts makes the struts interchangeable within their type and obviates the need for lettering or numbering of struts.

Right: Providing a means of allowing baseboard leg length adjustment. If baseboard legs are all the same length they will probably not require a slot as long as this; 3in (75mm) or so will provide all the adjustment that will ever be needed. These legs are for Yes Tor Junction, the baseboards for which are a bit of a three-dimensional maze, with no two legs the same length. This degree of adjustment has allowed some interchangeability between the legs.

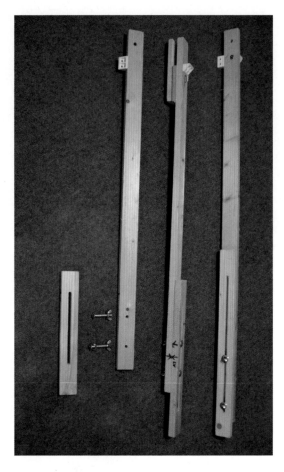

Far right: A trestle-type leg supporting part of the storage sidings behind Yes Tor Junction. Another advantage of trestle-type legs is that their height can easily be adjusted by altering the length of the string or chain holding together the bottom of the trestle. This is a great help when setting up a model railway in a gently sloping garden, as here.

baseboard legs attached higher up. These struts should be connected to the main legs by long bolts resting in holes drilled parallel to the larger cross-section of the legs.

If you intend to set your model railway up in a number of locations during its life, perhaps taking it to a few local exhibitions, any four-legged baseboards will really need some kind of length adjustment on the legs. This will enable them to be set up on the less than perfectly flat floors that always seem to exist in exhibition halls. A very simple way of providing such adjustment is shown below. In this case the slots were cut in the legs with a routing tool in a pillar drill; however, the same result could be achieved by drilling a series of holes along the leg and breaking out the wood left between them with a chisel.

If installing legs, bolts and braces individually every time a model railway is put up sounds a bit tedious, there is an alternative. The layout can be supported on stand-alone trestle legs which can simply be unfolded and the layout placed on top. While this erection procedure is undoubtedly more straightforward, the trestles themselves do take longer to construct than the simple leg-and-brace approach to layout elevation and (because they require more materials) they tend to be more expensive. The choice of leg type is really down to the individual and the situation.

sockets constructed as described above. Some form of check on the leg is required to take the weight of the board. I find screwing a plastic corner-joining plate to the leg is a simple and perfectly adequate way of achieving this.

I tend to build model railways so that track level is approximately at eye level if I am sitting in front of the layout. For me, this means the track should be approximately 45in (900mm) above the floor. The legs required beneath my model railways are, therefore, usually around 4ft long, the precise length depending upon the depth of the baseboard.

If the baseboards are narrow (less than about 300mm wide) and light, as often the case for non-scenic curves at either end of an oval model railway, a single leg can be used for support. For wider or heavier baseboards elevated 4ft above ground level a sturdier form of baseboard support structure is required. Legs should be provided on either side of the baseboard and should be braced together to avoid the layout swaying about in an alarming fashion. Timber of 1in x ½in (25mm x 12mm) is ideal for bracing construction. A horizontal strut should be provided at low level – 6in (150mm) or so above the floor – and a diagonal strut between pairs of

Baseboard joints

When more than one baseboard is used it is necessary to develop a method for holding adjacent baseboards together. The easiest way to do this is to bolt them to each other using a pair of nuts and bolts at each joint, resting in pre-drilled holes in the baseboard end. I usually use wingnuts rather than hexagonal nuts, as they are easier to tighten by hand. It is also worth drilling the holes a millimetre or two larger than the bolt diameter. This enables the location of the boards relative to each other to be finely adjusted to ensure that the rail ends line up. Once this has been done the bolts can be tightened, locking the boards in position.

An alternative to having to line the rails up across all the baseboard joints is to use a pair of locating devices, such as brass patternmaker's dowels, at each rail joint. These are essentially a brass spigot and corresponding socket which are manufactured to fit accurately within each other. They can usually be picked up at large railway exhibitions or from baseboard material suppliers. A set of bolts is still used to hold the board together, although the alignment function is undertaken by the dowels. This makes putting up the railway a quicker and easier process, but it does require the dowels to be carefully inserted into the ends of the baseboards, which can be a bit of a fiddly task. The easiest method is to clamp together the ends of both baseboards abutting the joint and to drill the holes for the dowels through the ends of both baseboards at

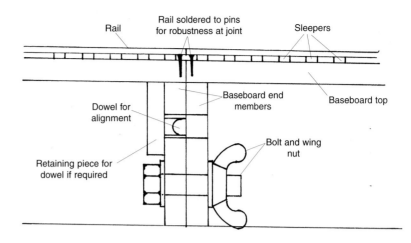

the same time. If these are constructed in thin plywood the dowels are unlikely to gain sufficient grip to keep them in place, so an undrilled backing plate should be glued on the rear of the baseboard end covering the rear of the dowels to hold them securely.

Once the baseboards have been constructed the foundations of your model railway are in place. It is surprising how satisfying it can be to set out the track for the first time on a freshly built baseboard and imagine what the completed layout will look like. However, once you have laid the track out temporarily a few times and got used to its appearance the desire to get the track down permanently will increase. How this is best achieved is discussed in the next chapter.

Above: A section through the joint between two baseboards. The joint is held together by a wing nut and bolt, and the alignment maintained by a pattern-maker's dowel.

5 Laying the Track

Right: Luxulyan, Cornwall, 1957. The trackwork shown here is typical of the real railway: one curve flows into another and there are no sudden changes in radius or direction. By planning ahead and carefully choosing turnouts from the various ranges available, pre-fabricated track can easily be made to look this good. *A. Attewell*

When making your first tentative steps from a train set on the lounge floor to the heady world of model railway ownership there is no need to lay out large sums of money on new track. Exactly the same track can be used. However, there are two main differences when laying the track for a model railway in comparison to setting out a train set on the floor. Firstly, model railway track will need to be stuck down onto a baseboard. It is important that this process is undertaken carefully as poorly laid track will give bad running for the life of the layout. Secondly, model railway track is usually built into a scenic landscape, which means that a representation of the ballast beneath the track will be required.

When constructing their first model railway, I would imagine that most people will be intending to use track straight out of the packet. I believe that this is a very sensible approach. It is certainly possible to make your own track, and some extremely realistic-looking model railways can be constructed if this is done. However, this is a time-consuming and complicated process, and it is very difficult to construct track which will run as well as that which can be bought over the counter of your local model shop.

Types of model railway track

A vast array of different types and sizes of track is now available in the common model-railway gauges, both for plain track and for points and crossings.

Generally, manufacturers produce two distinct ranges of points and crossings, one aimed more at the train set market, which incorporates sharp curves and turnout angles, and the other for the discerning model railway builder, with much flatter curves and a reduced crossing angle.

Plain track is also often sold in two forms: shorter pre-formed straight or curved sections and longer sections which can be gently flexed to almost any shape required. The geometry of the pre-formed track available has been carefully thought through so that almost any collection of pieces of track will fit together, and when a circuit is constructed it will almost always be possible to get the two ends to meet. This type of track is also often provided with fishplates already *in situ*, ready for installation on a layout.

Flexible track often requires cutting to length and the addition of fishplates which have been purchased separately. However, it can be laid to a radius much closer to that used for real

dimensioned track, which has a slightly smaller rail and is a better true-scale representation of railway track. If a large amount of older stock is to be run on a model railway the finer track should be used with caution, as trains with older, coarser wheels will tend to run along the rail fastenings and sleepers rather than the rails. The choice between these two types of track is really up to the individual. I have used fine Code 75 track on Gorran, but the same layout could easily have been built with traditional Code 100 track, the number relating in each case to the height of the rail in thousandths of an inch.

When purchasing turnouts, one further choice must be made between those with a 'live frog' and those with a 'dead frog'. Being the son of a railwayman of more years than he cares to

Left: A challenge to the model-railway builder: Waterloo station in Southern Railway days. If the connection from the left-hand platform to the second track from the left were omitted and the whole thing stretched out ever so slightly, this fantastically complex piece of trackwork could be recreated in products purchased straight from the model shop.

railway track. The real thing is actually laid out on very flat curves indeed, and even the tightest curves on the railway network are surprisingly gradual when scaled down to common model-railway dimensions. The curve at the London end of Southampton Tunnel is an example of one that even British Rail considered tight. In 4mm scale, however, the radius of the curve would be about 80in or 2m. This is about a quarter as tight as the flattest pre-formed curve available and is flatter than the 60in-radius curve in the main line of Gorran, which looks fairly flat for a model railway.

All the types of track mentioned above can be freely intermingled and attached together. However, care should be taken to ensure that, in instances such as the installation of turnouts to form a crossover between two parallel straight lines, the crossing angle of the two turnouts used matches. The short, sharp turnouts sold with train sets often have a crossing angle of 22½°, whereas longer, flatter turnouts, which to my mind look far more realistic and run much better, usually have a crossing angle of 11¼°. Using one of each type of turnout for a crossover would therefore result in a mismatched and awkward piece of trackwork with a nasty kink either in the main line or in the middle of the crossover.

In some scales the modeller has two further types of track from which to choose, these being the traditional pattern which has been in use for many years and a recently updated finer-

Left: The approach to Casterbridge station. The flowing curves of the main line have been created in part by careful selection of pointwork and the use of curved turnouts where appropriate. The railway-like look of the layout is the result of many hours spent investigating real railway track plans and thinking with the mindset of a 19th-century railway engineer.

Above: Prototypical turnouts at Norton Fitzwarren — the three-way junction just outside Taunton where the GWR lines to Exeter, Barnstaple and Minehead diverged. As can be seen, the crossing angle of the turnouts in use on the main line of the real railway is often very flat, as is the radius of curves, and this makes the turnouts quite lengthy. Turnouts produced for use on model railways are all much shorter than a true-scale representation of those shown in this photograph; for a realistic-looking layout the longest and flattest turnouts possible should be employed. *A. Attewell*

Right: The anatomy of a turnout. The upper and lower rails on the left-hand side of this drawing are of opposite electrical polarities, to supply electricity to the trains. As can be seen, the two polarities come into contact at the crossing, which could create a short circuit unless carefully managed. The live- and dead-frog turnout systems have been devised to overcome this problem.

remember, I rather baulk at the use of the term 'frog' (we don't call the bit of a point where the rails cross a 'frog' on this side of the Atlantic; it's a crossing!), but, whatever the terminology, the distinction between the two is worthy of explanation.

Due to the fact that the two rails which intersect at a crossing are of opposite electrical polarities, some kind of electrical solution has to be employed to prevent a short circuit. One way

of overcoming this is not to have the two rails crossing but to stop them short of each other and create the crossing itself in plastic. This is the 'dead frog' system. All the necessary wiring is built into the turnouts at the factory, so no thought is really required by the modeller when wiring up these turnouts.

'Live frog' turnouts have an all-metal crossing, and the polarity of this is switched depending on which way the point is set. This switching can be achieved by the point blades or by a separate switch on a point motor, if one is fitted. Insulating fishplates are required on the two rails leading from the crossing, and some wiring will probably be needed in order to take power around the turnout for the trains on either side of it. All the necessary wiring is explained in the instructions supplied with the turnouts.

The choice between dead- and live-frog

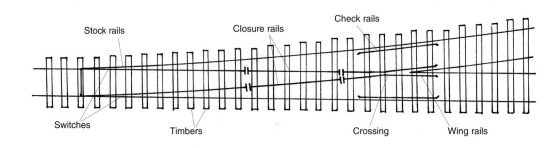

turnouts is a matter for the individual. Some short-wheelbase locomotives can struggle when crossing a dead-frog turnout, as there will be no power supplied to a wheel while it is passing over the plastic part of the crossing. Often this is not a problem, and if the extra wiring required with live-frog turnouts is definitely not your cup of tea I would recommend taking the risk of occasional locomotive stalling. However, if you wish to do everything in your power to promote smooth running and do not mind doing some extra wiring, then live-frog turnouts are definitely recommended.

Marking out the track

Once you have decided upon a track layout and tried it out on the floor a few times, it is time to get the track stuck down and begin constructing the rest of the model railway around it.

The first step is to lay the track out on the baseboard to check that it fits. This dry run also allows you to play around with the layout and its position on the board, making sure that all the buildings you want to include fit in.

If you are using flexible track, I recommend resisting the urge to cut it neatly to the correct length just yet. It is better to wait until the track is actually being pinned down so that you are absolutely certain that it is cut in the correct place. Complete lengths of flexible track can usually be bent to a close enough approximation of any curves that are required to ensure the layout will fit on the board.

Once the layout has been positioned where you want it on the board the track alignment should be marked. The centrelines of the individual tracks can be marked in pencil between the sleepers. The location of the buildings is also worth marking; otherwise they will never quite go back in the place you had in mind. It is important, of course, that sufficient clearance be left between buildings and railway lines for the trains to pass, particularly on curved track, where parts of coaches will overhang the track further than may be expected.

Once the locations of all the various features have been transferred to the baseboard the track and buildings can be removed to allow the ballast to be laid.

Below: Marking around the water tower.

Right: Foam ballast inlay for plain line. Supplied on a roll, it can be simply unrolled and located around the sleepers to create the impression of ballast.

Below right: When spraying foam ballast the spray can should be held about a foot from the target area so that only a thin mist of paint actually reaches the foam, the objective being to change its grey colour to that of natural stone. The edge of the ballast on the left has also been distressed slightly with a pair of scissors. Unadulterated ballast is shown on the right for comparison.

Below: Use of a pre-formed ballast inlay unit for a turnout. If the turnout is to be mechanically or electrically operated, remember to cut an opening in the inlay for the mechanism. The large hole towards the top of the photograph is for a signal.

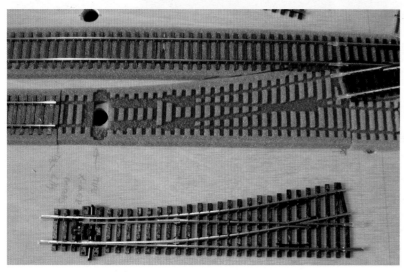

Ballasting

There are a number of ways in which ballast can be represented on a model railway. The choice between them depends on the location of the track in question and the preference of the modeller.

Pre-formed foam inlay can be used to good effect to represent ballast, particularly for main-line tracks. This is supplied on a roll. Once the track is nailed down the ballast will be retained in position.

Using foam ballast straight off the roll results in extremely regimented ballast 'shoulders' (the edges sloping down to baseboard or ground level). These are really a bit too orderly, even for a well-tended main line, and to overcome this the edge of the foam can be distressed using a pair of scissors or a modelling knife before it is laid beneath the track. Some variation in the colour of the ballast can also be introduced by spraying the foam from a distance with brown spray paint.

When it comes to points and crossings it is possible carefully to cut the plain track inlay to suit the diverging tracks. However, it is much easier to buy the specially shaped inlays available for the majority of turnout types. These are supplied in packs of two.

Foam ballast also elevates the track above board level, which is not very prototypical in goods yards and sidings, where the upper surface of the sleepers was usually at ground level. For true realism another form of ballasting is necessary in these locations.

Fine stone, in a range of sizes and materials, can be used to represent railway ballast. Products to mimic cinders or blast-furnace slag are also available and can be useful for ballasting sidings or yard surfaces. An unusual material which can be extremely useful when installing yard surfaces is dried mud. Ordinary garden mud should be dried out for a few hours in a biscuit tin in the oven on a low heat (preferably when the owner of the oven is out), ground down and sieved to produce a fine powder. When this is mixed with fine stone or cinders a realistic-looking surface can be created.

When using the loose-ballast technique the track can be laid directly onto the baseboard. However, as the track will be locked into place on the baseboard, this will tend to amplify the sound of the trains, resulting in a very noisy model railway. It is better to lay the track on a layer of something forgiving like cork flooring tiles, which will provide some sound insulation. This will also raise the track and the surrounding

Above: The level crossing and part of the yard at St Clears, West Wales. The level of the ground in the yard is similar to that at the crossing, almost at rail head level. Foam ballast would not provide a particularly realistic representation of this ground surface; use of loose fine stone and mud glued together with diluted glue once marshalled into place would be the best way to tackle a surface like this. Notice how the moving switch rails of the turnouts have been left unballasted; this should also be done on a model to allow the turnout to continue to operate correctly. *A. Attewell*

Above: Laying cork flooring tiles to provide a raised ground level in the engine shed and yards. A layer of scrap cardboard is placed between the cork and the books, the weight of which is being used to prevent the corners of the cork tiles turning up; sometimes PVA seeps up the edges of the tiles, which will not improve the front covers of these nice large hardbacks!. A large brush is ideal for applying the glue to an extensive area such as this.

Above: Flooding loosely laid ballast with glue on Gorran. The ballast in the yard is a mixture of 'cinders' ballast and dried mud, which is laid dry around the track by marshalling it into position with a fingertip and the two paintbrushes (one firm, one soft) shown. The bottle contains the mixture described above and is used to drip the diluted glue into position.

Above: A down-at-track-level shot of Gorran. The yard surface has been installed as described above, with the top of the ballast level with the tops of the sleepers.

ground level to more or less the same level as track laid on foam underlay, which is helpful if both methods of ballasting are employed on a layout.

When ballasting track with loose ballast it is easiest to install the track first and to place the ballast around the track while it is dry, carefully marshalling it into position with a dry paintbrush. Once you are happy with the location of the ballast it can be glued into place

by gently dripping watered-down PVA glue onto it. A mixture of approximately one part glue to five parts water is required. A small drop of washing-up liquid and a drop of light-grey acrylic paint should also be added to the mix. The washing-up liquid reduces surface tension in the diluted glue, which could otherwise prevent it flowing properly through the ballast, while the grey paint prevents the PVA from making the ballast look shiny. The mixture will take a couple

Right: The goods yard at Thame in 1960, with ballast up to the sleepers and beyond. Here brickwork has been used to provide a hard surface where the access road crosses a siding. This interesting feature could easily be represented in model form by using some brick-embossed plastic sheet, carefully cut to size, and then ballasting up to the level of the top of the sheet with loose stone and mud. *A. Attewell*

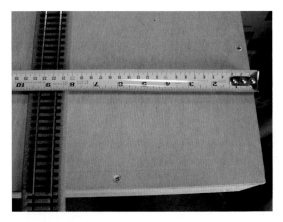

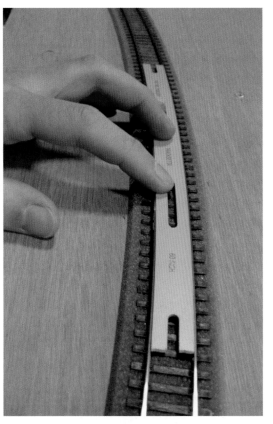

Far left: Using a tape to ensure that the first track to be laid, in this case the almost straight down main line, is parallel to the edge of the board.

Left: Using a Tracksetta template to set out an even 60in-radius curve. The slots which allow partial insertion of the track pins are clearly visible. Notice how flat this curve appears, yet it is still sharper than a scale version of Southampton Tunnel curve, which is considered very sharp by railwaymen.

of days to dry, but it is by far the easiest way of installing ballast to the full depth of the sleepers and of making sure the ballast ends up in the right place.

When installing a surface away from the track with fine loose material, stone or mud can simply be dusted onto a thin layer of PVA glue. This has been done for some of the yard surface at Gorran. Care should be taken if both methods of installation are used in one yard area, as the colour of the final ballast (once dry) will inevitably be slightly different depending on which method of installation was used.

The track-laying process
(i) Positioning the track
It is a good idea to start the track-laying process with a line which travels the full length of a baseboard, ideally a straight track or one at a constant curve. There is no actual need for railway track to be laid parallel to the edge of a baseboard, but laying track *almost* parallel tends to look like it has just been laid wrongly. If you find your main lines are about five degrees or less from parallel to the edge of the board

Left: The beautifully flowing trackwork of the real thing, in this case at Clunderwen in West Wales. The vast majority of the railway line in Great Britain is laid on a curve, much of it a very flat curve such as this, which can be replicated on model railways by careful use of flexible track.
A. Attewell

I recommend rotating the layout to enable the line to be built an equal distance from the edge of the board along its length.

When laying flexible track on a curve the only way to get a nice even curve is by using a template. I find the 'Tracksetta' templates particularly good, as they are available in a useful range of radii. These sit between the rails and include slots which allow track pins to be driven most of the way in with the template still in place, which ensures the track is fixed in exactly the correct position.

If you want your trackwork to look good and your model railway to look convincing, it is

Right: Cutting a piece of track with a piercing saw. Fine blades (with at least 56 teeth per inch — TPI) should be used for this task, or the saw will snag on the rail. These blades are prone to breaking whilst in use, but they are very cheap, and the frame of the saw is designed to allow easy replacement of broken blades.

Above: Drilling a hole for a track pin in a sleeper. A micro-drill is the tool for the job. A set of these, as shown, can be picked up at an exhibition if not available in the local model shop, and they are surprisingly useful tools. Here the author is using a miniature Archimedes drill, which tends to be a bit more gentle with the delicate drill bits than are the alternative types.

important that the trackwork flow nicely from one curve to the next curve or straight. The trains will actually run around some quite horrendous kinks in model trackwork, but the eye is much less tolerant. It is important to get your eye as close as possible to track level (even if this involves a few contortions of the body!) in order to observe the flow of the track and make corrections where necessary.

(ii) Cutting and fixing the track

When it comes to cutting the track there are a variety of specialised rail cutters available, and these work well when the blades are sharp. However, as soon as the cutting edge becomes blunt the cut becomes much less clean, making it difficult to slide the fishplates onto the end of a piece of track. If you can afford to replace these cutters every time they start to become blunt they are probably the best option. However, I find it easier and much less taxing on the wallet to use a small piercing saw to cut the track to the required length.

The place where the cut is required should be marked, with the track *in situ*, by making a small nick on the railhead with a needle file or similar. It is important to consider how the sleepers will fit around the final joint, as it always looks best if a rail joint occurs in the middle of a normally-sized gap between two sleepers. Once marked, the track can be cut through using a piercing saw or rail cutters. When cutting track with a piercing saw it is sensible to fashion a block of hardwood to hold the track firmly whilst it is being cut and eliminate any risk of the saw slipping and cutting through your fingers. However, with care, track can also be cut on the edge of the baseboard.

Once cut to size, the track is ready to be fixed down to the baseboard. It is possible to glue the track into the ballast as you glue the ballast in place, but it is difficult to get the track in the correct position using this process. It is also almost impossible to make small alterations to the alignment of the track once the glue has dried. It is much better to pin the track down with some nails. The type of nail used depends on the characteristics of the wood used as the trackbase. If it is made from Sundeala board (or similar) thin track pins can be used as the surface of the board is relatively soft, and they can more or less be pushed in by hand. If the trackbase is made from plywood the surface will be much tougher, and thin track pins are likely to bend while being hammered in place. Very small veneer pins are a better alternative in this case,

Above: A good technique for installing track pins without endangering fingers! The pin can be gently held vertical and hit squarely with the hammer.
The author prefers to use a large hammer for this kind of task, using absolutely no force and allowing the weight of the tool to do the work. A smaller hammer such as that also shown in this photograph can be used with softer baseboards like those made from Sundeala board. A nail punch can be used to drive the last little bit of track pin down below rail level without risk of hitting and bending the rails with the hammer.

although track pins may still be preferred, as they are less visually intrusive. It is desirable to drill a small hole in each sleeper that will be nailed down rather than trying to drive a track pin through an undrilled sleeper and running the risk of splitting the sleeper in two. Be careful also not to drive the track pins too far into the baseboard, particularly if the track is being installed on compressible foam underlay, as this risks breaking the rail housings and ripping the sleeper from the rails.

BROKEN RAIL HOUSING

Above: The result of driving a nail too far through a plastic sleeper whilst the sleeper is resting on foam. The clip holding the far rail to the sleeper has been pulled off the rail by the force of the nail being inserted. This is very unsightly in an otherwise neat stretch of track.

(iii) Fishplates

Model railway track is fixed together using rail joiners or (to give them their proper name) fishplates. Two types are available: conductive fishplates, made from nickel silver, and insulating, moulded from clear plastic.

Sometimes the end of a rail will burr over during the cutting process, making it difficult or impossible to slide a fishplate onto the end of the rail. If this happens, some gentle filing with a needle file is needed to restore the rail to its normal shape. The fishplate can then be slid into place. Gentle force is often needed to slide fishplates onto the end of rails, but too much force can damage the track. It is particularly important to be careful when forcing a fishplate onto a rail in a turnout, as sometimes this can make the turnout rails move, meaning the point blades will not sit correctly against the stock rail. If this does happen, gently pull the stock rail back into position with a pair of pliers.

Pre-formed track usually comes with conductive fishplates ready-fixed to the rail ends by small spot welds. Flexible track does not come

Above: Conductive fishplates for Code 75 track. Code 100 fishplates are very similar and are also used for 'O'-gauge track. The fishplates are supplied in pairs, as shown on the left; with a few flexes between the fingers these will snap into single plates.

Above: Insulating fishplates. These are supplied in threes, as on the left, and require a bit of careful knifework to liberate the individual units.

Left: Sleepers trimmed back to allow the correct sleeper spacing to continue right up to a turnout. In this case (where a short-radius turnout has been used) it has been necessary to trim the ends of the first three sleepers after the joint. I have trimmed a small amount of the sleepers of both tracks to keep things looking even. Trimmed rail housings, to allow the fishplates to fit over the sleepers, can also be discerned.

with fishplates attached, and these will need to be purchased separately. Sometimes, for electrical reasons, it is necessary to replace a conductive fishplate supplied on a pre-formed turnout with an insulating fishplate. The least-difficult way I have found of removing these (notice I have not said easiest; this can be a tricky task) involves a two-stage process. Firstly, the sides of the fishplate should be levered up using a screwdriver. Pliers are then required to waggle the fishplate until the weld breaks. The fishplate can then be removed.

When introducing a fishplated joint into what used to be a continuous piece of flexible track it is important to trim the rail housings off the last sleeper before the joint. This can be done with a knife, making sure your fingers will not be in the way if the knife slips. This will allow the fishplates, which are longer than the space between two sleepers, to fit snugly over the top of the sleepers on either side of the joint.

When two tracks converge at a turnout the ends of the sleepers from each track often clash. The solution to this is to use a sharp knife to trim the ends of the sleepers in question, cutting off a small amount at a time and reassembling the joint at regular intervals to check if enough has been removed.

(iv) Baseboard joints

Model railway track is surprisingly robust, particularly in terms of its ability to resist a load placed directly on top of it. However, it is quite vulnerable at the edges of baseboards when the layout is stored out of use, and it is easy to catch

a rail end with a sleeve or a shoe and rip a considerable length of rail from its housing. It is therefefore recommended that the rails at the ends of the baseboards be fixed solidly to the baseboard itself. This can be a fiddly task, but it is well worth doing.

The easiest way is to drive a panel pin into the edge of the baseboard and solder the rail to this pin, as shown in the diagram of a baseboard joint at the end of Chapter 4. To do this the track should be laid right up to a board joint, the alignment checked, and the position of the centrelines of the rails marked on the baseboard.

Below: Forming the final connection between a panel pin and the rail at a baseboard joint. A soldering iron is being applied to the previously tinned elements of the joint, and the whole is melted together to form one solid mass. With a bit of careful soldering, a strong and unobtrusive joint can be created.

The rails should then be moved aside while the panel pins are driven into the baseboard to the correct height.

The plastic webbing between the sleepers should be removed from the track with a knife, which may require the track to be separated temporarily from the baseboard. The bottom of the rail should then be cleaned and tinned with solder. The top of the panel pin should also be cleaned, with a needle file or emery paper, and tinned. Once this is done the track can be put back in place and the alignment adjusted until it is correct. The two tinned surfaces can then be joined into one solid soldered joint by re-applying the soldering-iron to melt the joint together. For more detail on the soldering process readers are refer to the next chapter, which discusses model-railway electrics.

(v) Electrification

Models of modern prototype locations in many parts of the country would be incomplete without a representation of the methods used to supply electricity to electric trains, be it through use of a third rail (often referred to as the conductor rail or 'con rail') or overhead line equipment. Both systems can be represented in model form, and such representations can be very helpful when creating the impression of a particular region or line. A model of Crewe station in the Rail-blue era, for example, would look very bare without a network of overhead electrical wiring (often termed 'the knitting' by railwaymen).

At the time of writing there is a gap in the market when it comes to ready-to-use overhead-electrification masts and ancillary equipment in the UK. However, there are rumours that this is about to be filled. Until this occurs, use of some of the components manufactured for Continental layouts is recommended.

Representing the Southern Railway's third-rail system or the outpost of this system found around Liverpool can be easily achieved using Code 60 rail and the kits of model insulator 'pots' that are available. The latter should be inserted in holes drilled in the ends of every fourth sleeper, as recommended in the instructions that come with the kit. Care should be taken when planning on which side of the track to install the third rail. As usual, careful study of the prototype is recommended; for example, it is very unusual for the third rail to be located directly adjacent to a platform.

Once all the track has been installed on a model railway (or even on just one baseboard) the desire to get it wired up, so that the trains can be run, increases dramatically. This process is described in the next chapter.

Right: Third-rail electrification does not take long to install: simply drill a hole in every fourth sleeper, add a plastic 'pot', and thread the rail in place. The normal method in open running line, as here, is for the rails to overlap but in pointwork, gaps can be provided, as an electric train has more than one shoe with which to pick up the current. Con rail should not end part way along a turnout: it should either go right past it or stop short of it. As shown here, the conductor rail periodically swaps sides of the track to allow expansion of the rail.

Left: An old 'centre off' analogue controller. When the speed knob is in the central position the trains are stopped. Turning the knob in either direction increases the speed of the trains in one direction or the other.

Below: Wiring diagram for more modern types of analogue controller which require a separate transformer. Most modern controllers need a 16V AC supply, but it is worth checking: there are a few out there, such as the old Scalespeed controllers, which work on 12V DC.

Like it or not, model railways need electricity. However, the wiring is an aspect about which people often feel particularly nervous, and which can even prevent them from embarking on the enterprise altogether. This, I think, is a shame. Although model railways can be wired up with miles of wire and have control panels constructed with all manner of switches and coloured lights, there is no actual need for this. They can, in fact, be wired up in a very simple way.

There are now two systems which can be used to control the speed and direction of model trains.

The traditional system of varying the voltage in the rails is usually referred to as the 'analogue' system. A transformer is used to convert mains supply of 240V AC to around 12V DC, which what the trains need. This transformer is often mounted within a 'controller', which, by varying the output voltage to the track, allows the speed of the trains to be adjusted. Older controllers usually have a knob which turns in both directions, corresponding to the direction of travel, the supply to the track being 'off' when the indicator on the knob is pointing towards the top of the controller. A controller of this type is shown in the figure above. More-modern analogue controllers often have a switch which controls the direction of the

trains and a separate speed knob. The direction switch usually has three settings – one for each direction of travel and a central 'off' position (which can often be selected accidentally selected and leaves you wondering why the trains won't run!). Some modern controllers, such as those supplied for hand-held use, incorporate only the electronics required to set train speed and direction and require a separate transformer to change the mains voltage into the voltage required by the controller.

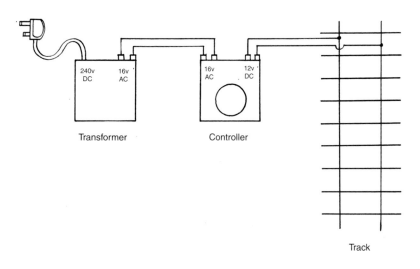

Transformer   Controller   Track

Above: Power clips supplying electricity to the track. Most model railways could be powered by these and nothing else.

Below right: An under-the-board connection between single-core wire (on the left) and flex (right) leading to the controller. These screw connectors or 'chocolate blocks' are an easy way of joining wires together. I have discovered (whilst trying to trace more wiring faults than I care to remember) that you can never identify wires too clearly under a railway board, which is the reason for the written identification and the connection numbering. This relates back to a connection list detailing the direction of each wire and what it is connected to at the other end.

In order to operate more than one train using analogue control it is necessary to employ isolating switches to turn various sections of track (and hence various locomotives) on and off. However, such arrangements have in recent years been rendered superfluous by Digital Command Control (DCC), which has applied state-of-the-art technology to the world of railway modelling and in so doing has reduced the complexity of the wiring required to run an extensive layout.

Under the digital system a transformer is used to provide the entire track layout with a constant supply. A single digital controller enables the operator to operate any locomotive on a layout by sending out control instructions (such as 'reverse' or 'slow down') which are transmitted through the rails. All locomotives on the layout are fitted with a decoder chip, each with a unique 'address' which is included in any instruction sent by the controller; only the

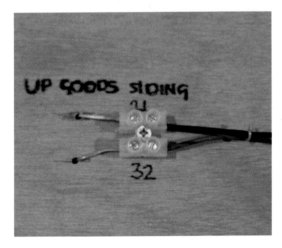

locomotive with that 'address' will respond to a particular instruction, and each can therefore be controlled individually, anywhere on the layout. Fitting a decoder to every locomotive can be an expensive exercise, as the decoders are not cheap, but they can be used to control a variety of additional functions such as remote control of the red and white lights at either end of the locomotive. They also allow refinements such as fitting speakers to each locomotive to emit prototypical sounds, which can add an extra dimension to an otherwise mute model.

DCC undoubtedly reduces the amount of wiring required to operate a model railway, but it is not cheap – and it does enable you to drive trains directly into one other if you are not paying close attention! If it sounds tempting I would refer you the Ian Allan book on the subject, details of which can be found under 'Recommended Reading'. Intended for those to whom DCC does not appeal, the remainder of this chapter is concerned with the operation of model trains by means of conventional analogue control.

Connections to the track

On an analogue-control system all the trains need to run is a positive electrical supply from the controller to one rail and a negative supply from the controller to the other rail, and away they will go. The arrangement required is exactly the same whether you are laying out a train set on the floor or constructing a model railway on a baseboard. In both instances the use of power clips is the simplest way of connecting an electrical supply to the rails.

The trouble with power clips is that they can be visually quite intrusive. Whilst this is less of a problem if the track is laid out on the floor, it is a shame to have a great big plastic lump, with a couple of wires leading to it ,slap bang in the middle of an otherwise beautifully crafted and realistic-looking model railway.

An alternative way of getting power to the rails is to wrap a wire around a fishplate and then pass it through a hole in the baseboard. Thin wire is best in this situation, as a thicker wire can create an obstruction to the flange of the wheels as they pass, causing trains to bump over the joint to which the wires are connected. Single-core electrical cable culled from telephone or networking cable is ideal, as it holds its shape well and can be wrapped tightly around the fishplates. 'Bell wire' (plastic-coated twin-core wire, as used for doorbells) is also suitable.

If the length of wiring back to the controller is more than a couple of feet it is desirable to change from thin single-core wire to a more-robust flexible wire; over time the wiring will inevitably get moved about, and in such circumstances single-core wire tends to snap inside its plastic coating. Therefore, a connection between the flex and the single-core wire attached to the rail needs to be arranged beneath the baseboard, and this can easily be achieved using a simple connector block.

The method of twisting wires around fishplates and connecting them together in screw connector blocks will allow you to wire up just about any layout. However, such connections are sometimes prone to breaking: the wire twisted around the fishplates can sometimes come loose, and the screw connector blocks can bite the end off a section of flex as the screws are done up. The answer to both of these problems is to use soldered connections. This method allows wires to be soldered solidly onto the rails and allows the end of lengths of flex to be soldered or 'tinned' into one solid piece of metal, which screw connector blocks are less prone to breaking.

If some people are slightly wary of electrics there are many more who are worried about the idea of soldering; but this, I feel, is unjustified. Whilst it is perfectly possible to build and operate a model railway without soldering, it really is worth giving it a try.

All that is really important (the absolute golden rule) is that the pieces of metal that you are soldering are clean. When soldering wiring together this is not too much of a problem as any new wire will be quite clean. The rule is more important when you are soldering onto a piece of rail or a switch. In these instances it is likely that the area you intend to solder onto will need a quick bit of attention with a file or some emery paper to remove the naturally occurring oxide layer.

Flux is a chemical which aids the soldering process by getting the metal really clean when you heat it up with the soldering-iron. I advise its use for every soldered joint. Some fluxes sold for use with steel can actually rust the metal if not washed off after soldering, and I tend, therefore, to use brass flux for everything, including steel if and when appropriate.

Flux can be bought as a liquid or a paste. The method of application will differ depending on the form it takes, but the tip of a cocktail stick or an old paintbrush is usually used to apply a very small amount of flux to the place it is needed.

When forming a soldered joint the first step is to 'tin' both elements that are to be joined together. Tin is one of the two main constituent parts in solder (the other is lead), and I presume

this is where the expression comes from. Tinning involves applying a thin layer of solder to both elements individually before they are brought together. The soldering-iron is then applied once again in order to form the joint.

As well as tinning the wire you should also attend to the rail. It is usually easiest to solder onto rails from underneath, which also means that the final joint will be completely hidden in the ballast. The first step is to remove the web joining the sleepers together over a short length and then clean the foot of the rail with a couple of passes by a fine file to get it nice and shiny.

Once both rail and wire are tinned they can be soldered together. All that is required is another brush of flux onto the tinned bit of the rail, and then both elements are held together. The iron is then reapplied, usually to the wire, as this will be on top. As the iron is placed onto the wire the solder in the wire melts. The solder on

Above: Tinning a piece of flex. The insulation is stripped off the end, and all the individual strands are given a quick twist together to prevent any stragglers. A small amount of flux is applied to the wire and the soldering iron, and the solder and the wire are then brought together. The melted solder runs through the end of the wire by capillary action, which only takes a second or two. The soldering iron and the solder can then be removed from the freshly tinned piece of flex.

Left: Soldering flex to the foot of a rail. Both the rail and the wire have been tinned, and they are just about to be brought back together and the soldering iron reapplied. If the solder won't 'take' to the rail the latter probably is not clean enough.

the rail is then in contact with this molten solder, and it also melts. Once the heat is removed (a second or two after it is applied) the whole joint cools down as one piece of metal. If the joint is brittle and comes apart it can always be re-

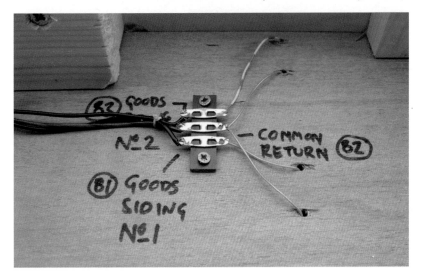

soldered. If it does this it was probably moved slightly too soon after the iron was removed, or the iron was not held in place for long enough.

Once the soldering technique has been mastered (a few practices on a scrap piece of track will help) it can be used in a variety of railway-modelling situations. My preferred technique for connecting wires together, for example, is to solder them onto little metal tags on an insulating board called a tagstrip. To do this, exactly the same steps as those described above should be followed. The wire is tinned, the tag on the tagstrip is cleaned and tinned, the wire is held on top of the tag and the whole joint is soldered solid.

Control of isolating sections

The techniques described above all enable a controller to be connected to a length of track and allow electricity to flow through the rails and power the trains. However, with only a little more work and no more electrical understanding than

Above: A joint between single-core wire from the track and flex leading to the controller, made using soldered connections on tagstrip. Tagstrip is supplied in rows of 28 tags but can be cut down easily to the desired size, and, by removing a tag, useful fixing holes can be created. Only three terminals are used here for four leads from the track, because two of them are on the same side of the track and can be connected together. They are connected back to the return side of the controller through a 'common return' wire carried around the layout like a ring main in a house. The positive rails of both sidings are carried back to individual isolating switches on the control panel.

Below: The locomotive line outside Gorran's engine shed, with a number of fine machines ready for duty. This is a location where electrical control of individual sections of track is particularly useful. Each locomotive here is standing on an individual isolating section, all about a foot long. Being able to control the locomotives individually means they can be stacked up in a siding like this and then released for duty one at a time, just as they would be in real life.

Left: A switch controlling an isolating section at the lineside. The two wires connecting the track to the switch can easily be seen. When the switch is 'on', electricity flows around the insulated fishplate (just above the black arrow), allowing the trains to run normally. When the flow of electricity through the switch is turned off, a locomotive standing beyond the insulated joint can be electrically isolated from the rest of the layout.

Left: A control panel grouping together four isolating switches, for ease of operation. The face of the control panel is white melamine-faced hardboard, on which the track layout has been drawn, using permanent marker pen, to allow the switches to be geographically located; an alternative is to use the thin tape sold in automotive shops to apply coach lining to cars. The switches used are 'doll's house' or tumbler switches which have screw terminals, as can just be seen in the examples on the left. There is therefore no need to purchase soldering equipment in order to include isolating sections on a layout, as wires can be attached to these switches with a screwdriver.

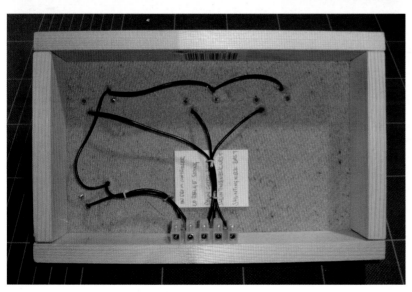

Left: The same control panel from behind. A simple frame of softwood has been constructed to give the panel some depth. The wiring to the switches has been collected together in a 'chocolate block' screw connector which facilitates easy connection to the layout, and each terminal is labelled on a piece of card glued to the back of the hardboard. As can be seen, only one 'supply' wire is used looped between switches. If only one controller is employed on a layout, as was the case here, this cuts down on the number of wires within the panel. The wires are held together for neatness by loops of single-core flex. This is wound around a bunch of wiring and twisted tight with pliers, almost inevitably snapping from over-tightening at the very last moment! A good alternative to avoid this problem is to use cable ties, which are very cheap and readily available.

Right: Use of a changeover section at the entrance to a goods yard. If a train is entering the yard from the main line the switch will initially be set to connect the changeover section to the main-line supply. The train will then be brought into the changeover section and stopped. (This is quite a normal operation in a goods yard, where the main-line driver will stop and await the instructions of the yard shunter.) The changeover switch will then be changed so that the section is controlled by the yard controller. The goods train can then be shunted whilst the main-line controller is free to run another main-line train.

Below: Use of a changeover switch to control a branch line. The switch can be set to connect the branch to either main line, depending on which way the train will travel across the junction.

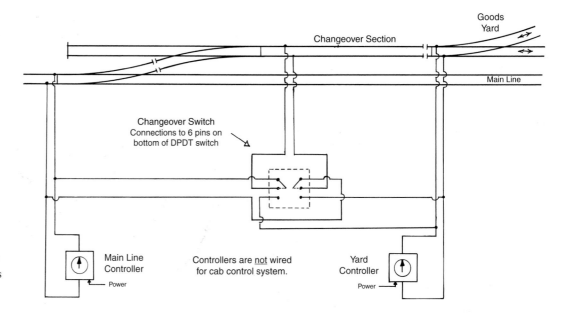

Changeover Section

Goods Yard

Main Line

Changeover Switch
Connections to 6 pins on bottom of DPDT switch

Main Line Controller

Power

Controllers are _not_ wired for cab control system.

Yard Controller

Power

DPDT = Double Pole Double Throw Switch

an awareness of how a torch works, the electrical system of a model railway can be made to do so much more.

The most useful thing that electrical control will allow you to do is to create isolating sections. These enable you to run a train onto a particular stretch of track (for example a siding or a loop), turn it off electrically, and then run something else. This can also be achieved to an extent by using the turnouts to control the electrical supply to the track, but there are many instances when it is useful to be able to turn a particular stretch of track on or off without having to change a point.

If a number of electrically isolating sections have been included in a layout then some kind of switching will be necessary to turn the various sections on and off. A simple on/off switch is all that is required, and this needs to be arranged so that when switched 'on' it will bridge around the insulated joint and supply power to the isolating section.

When a number of isolating sections are installed in a similar area the switches controlling them can be grouped together on a control panel. The wiring is arranged in exactly the same fashion; there is just less walking around involved to get to all the switches! An example of a control panel with four isolating switches (for the goods loops and banking-engine refuge sidings associated with the top of a long gradient up to a tunnel) is shown on the previous page.

Changeover switches

Once the basic principle of isolating sections has been mastered, a simple extension of the same technique can be used to provide what I have decided to call 'changeover control' for your trains. I must stress that this is not essential, and a perfectly enjoyable and respectable model railway can be constructed without such a thing. It does, however, allow an extra degree of control over the trains, which in turn can make the experience of operating a model railway more realistic and potentially more pleasurable.

Many model railways are operated from one controller, which simply controls all the trains and perhaps some isolating sections. This single-controller approach means that only one train can be separately controlled at once. If, for

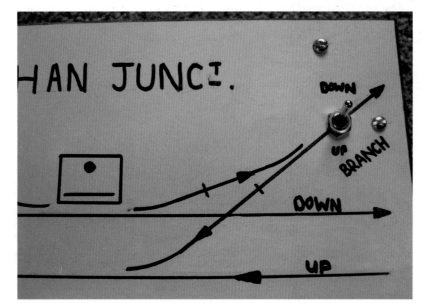

Above: A layout which could be controlled in just this manner, with a changeover switch deciding which of the two main lines is electrically connected to the branch (leading away to the right).

They cannot both be connected to the branch all the time as they would also therefore be connected to each other, rendering independent control of the two main lines impossible.

Above: Tinning a tag on a mini toggle switch. The soldering iron and solder are applied to the cleaned switch terminal at the same time.

arrangement is actually quite difficult to operate. The trains will quickly be transferred from one controller to the other as they pass the joint, resulting in a change in speed. If you forget to turn on one controller the train will come to a sudden stop, and if the controller is set in the opposite direction the train will stall at the boundary, shorting out both controllers.

From an operational point of view it is much better to have an electrical section between the goods yard and the main line, the control of which can be changed over between either controller. Such a section can be controlled by a changeover switch.

Other good examples of changeover switches in use include changing a colour-light signal from red to green or switching control of a branch line joining a double-track main line. In this case two controllers are likely to be used for the main lines (one for each track) so trains can tear past each other in opposite directions at different speeds. In lieu of a third controller for the branch a changeover switch can be used.

The switches normally used on model railways are 'miniature toggle' switches. Various types are available, for example DPDT (double-pole, double-throw) or SPST (single-pole, single-throw) switches.

The number of 'poles' refers to the number of sets of contacts that the switch has. Switches with six terminals on the bottom (DPDT switches) have two independent sets of contacts, both of which

example, a train is travelling into the station it is not possible separately to control another train shunting in the goods yard, perhaps in the opposite direction or at a different speed. To do this another controller would be required. This is not a problem in itself, as a pair of insulating fishplates can be installed between the running line and the goods yard, and the controllers connected to the relevant sections. However, this

Right: Cab control in action. If double-throw switches with a 'centre off' position are used (*i.e.* switches with three positions), isolation of the cab control sections can be achieved with the same switch as that used to change the supply between controllers.

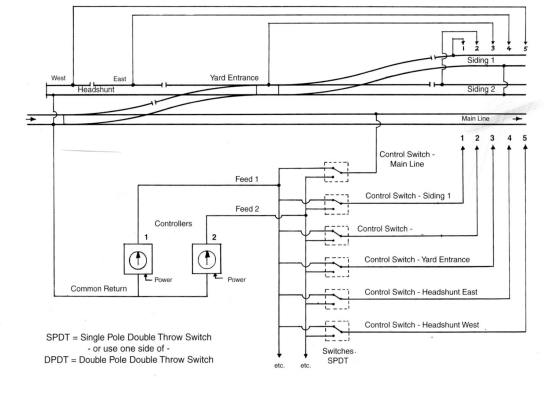

SPDT = Single Pole Double Throw Switch
- or use one side of -
DPDT = Double Pole Double Throw Switch

56

are operated by the switch lever. Single-throw switches have two contacts per pole, and the switch either connects the two contacts electrically or creates an electrical break between them, depending on which way the switch is thrown. In other words they are either 'on' or 'off'. The dolls'-house switches shown above are of the SPST type. Double-throw switches have three contacts per pole. One is a supply and the other two are the outputs from the switch. The supply will either be connected to one of the outputs or the other, depending which way the switch lever has been set. It is sometimes said that these switches are either 'on' or 'on', i.e. that they change the supply over between outputs. Double-pole, double-throw switches are used for arranging changeover control of a section of railway line.

Attaching wires to the switches requires soldering. As before, the switch terminals must be clean – a light pass with a fine file will do the job, or a quick rub with a bit of emery paper. The tag on the bottom of the switch and the wire will then require tinning. The tag will simply need a quick wipe of flux, then an application of the soldering-iron and some solder to it at the same time. It is easiest to do this when the switch is held in a vice.

Once the terminals of the switch have been tinned the wires can be tinned and attached to them by holding the tinned wire against the tinned terminal. The iron is then reapplied to re-melt the solder and, once the iron is removed, the whole lot will be fixed solid.

Cab control

Whereas the diagrams opposite have all shown the connections to both rails being switched, this is not actually necessary, provided that the two (or more) controllers have separate mains power supplies. A system called cab control can be used, which reduces the number of wires, insulated fishplates and poles on switches required.

Cab control will allow any number of sections to become changeover sections and to be controlled from one of a number of controllers. One rail must be chosen as a 'common' rail, which will not require any insulated fishplates for section isolation. The other rail will need to be split into individual electrical sections which will have their supply switched between controllers.

It is possible to buy controllers without the transformer which converts the mains voltage to 12V or 16V. These are usually called panel-

Below: The cab control switches and isolating section switches for Casterbridge. A clear colour-coded diagram is provided on the wall above the layout.

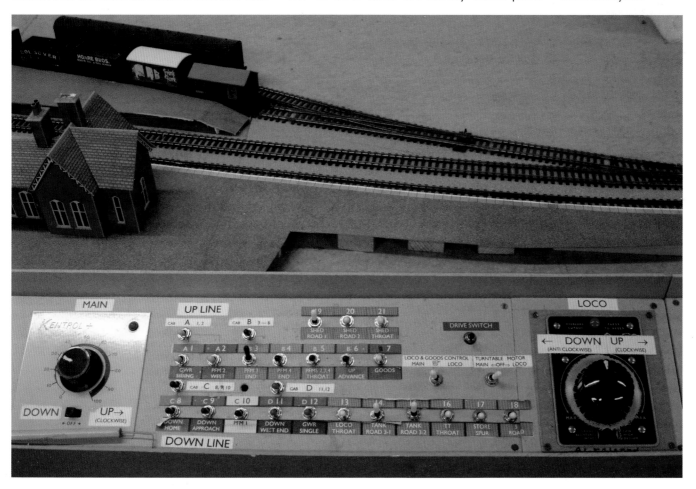

mounted controllers and are often slightly cheaper. If these are used, a separate mains transformer will be needed for each controller to allow cab control to work.

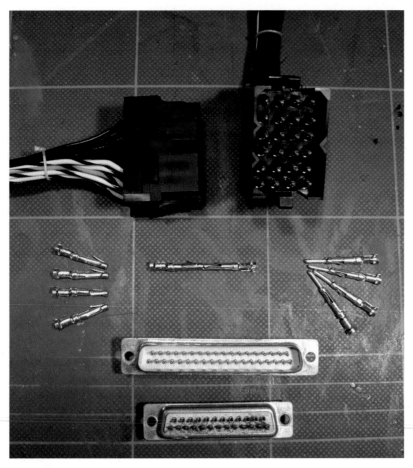

Above: Multi-pin plugs and sockets. At the foot of the photograph a pair of 'D' plugs are shown; these are cheaper than the alternative 24-way plug-and-socket sets but are smaller, more fiddly and less robust.

Baseboard joints

When constructing a model railway it is often necessary to carry wires across a joint between two baseboards in a way which allows the baseboards to be taken apart. If a very small number of wires cross the joint between boards, it is possible simply to carry wires across the joint each time the model railway is put up, attaching them to screw connectors mounted on each board. However, if more than a very few wires are carried across a baseboard joint, having to screw up and unscrew these connections every time the layout is put up or taken down becomes tiresome. It is far better, albeit slightly more expensive, to provide a plug-and-socket arrangement for the wires crossing a baseboard joint.

A large range of multi-pin plug-and-socket combinations are available. The 'D' plugs commonly used to attach and detach computer wiring are one option, although soldering onto the small pins used in these plugs can get a bit fiddly. My preference is for the multi-pin plug-and-socket type shown in the photograph left. The pins and plug-and-socket bodies for this type of plug are often sold separately and the modeller can add pins to the plugs as and when required. The pins are easy to solder on to and the plugs have a nice positive feel to them.

There are a large number of books available on the subject of model-railway wiring, which I recommend if this is an area which particularly interests you. A number of these appear in the 'Recommended Reading' list, including one discussing the control of model trains by DCC which will prove helpful if all the talk of sections and switches has left you somewhat confused!

Points and Signals 7

Points

Points (or turnouts) are an inherent part of almost any model railway, and there are a number of ways in which they can be operated. The simplest, obviously, is by hand, which is how all the points on my early model railways were operated. There is absolutely nothing wrong with this method, but as model-railway plans become increasingly complex it is often easier and more realistic not to have to walk over to a turnout in order to change it by means of a giant finger appearing from the sky!

The first turnout that I operated other than by hand was situated in a tunnel, where a single line split into double track. Evidently, in situations such as this some remote way of operating turnouts is desirable. Fortunately there are a number of options available. Either a mechanical link can be constructed from the turnout to a remote operating lever, or an electrical actuator (usually called a point motor by railwaymen) can be installed.

The choice between electrical or mechanical actuation is really down to the individual. Mechanical links are simpler to construct, as there is no need for a separate electrical supply or wiring to change the points. However, it is difficult to carry mechanical point control across a baseboard joint, which can be a problem on a large layout with lots of boards. The electrical option does not suffer this problem and is not complicated to arrange, especially as most model-railway controllers incorporate a 16V AC supply, which is ideal for turnout operation.

The easiest way to install remote mechanical operation of a turnout is to assemble a kit of parts. Ratio provides a particularly good one. A lever is supplied which is installed in a hole of 1/2in (13mm) diameter in the baseboard, and another 1/2in hole should be drilled beneath the tie-bar of the turnout. A brass extension piece is then screwed into the hole in the middle of the tie-bar, and a spring installed under the board, to pull the turnout in one direction. The lever is then linked to the turnout with a length of cord, which pulls the turnout against the spring, thus changing the points. A number of eyelets are usually supplied, allowing a few changes of direction in the cord between the lever and the turnout. The system can easily be extended with more eyelets and cord if required.

The most common type of point motor consists of a pair of electrical coils or solenoids, which when supplied with electricity form electromagnets and hence attract ferrous metals. The coils are usually wound around a tube and set up at either end of a piece of free-moving steel bar. As the coils are energised the bar is attracted in one direction or the other, and this motion is used to change the points. Electricity should be supplied for only a short time (a second or so), or the coils will heat up and melt. Special switches are therefore required to supply electricity to the point motor.

Point motors come in a variety of guises. Recently, surface-mounted motors, which clip onto the turnout, have become available again. These are extremely easy to wire up and use and are ideal in out-of-view locations, but they can be

Left: Mechanical control of turnouts in action. The brass stud is inserted through the hole in the baseboard and connects to the tie-bar of the point. The spring pulls the point one way, and the piece of linen thread pulls it the other when the point lever is operated.

Below left: In some situations a normal below-board point motor can be located above the baseboard within a building or hillside, as has been done here. This couples the ease of an above-board point-motor installation with reduced visual impact on a carefully detailed landscape. Peco manufactures a mounting plate complete with operating rod, which has been used here, to facilitate this kind of installation. If the operating rod is relatively long, it can be useful to install a couple of track pins on either side of the rod to keep it in alignment. If the heads of the pins are inserted to just clear the top of the rod they can help keep the operating rod on the spigot on the end of the tie-bar.

Right: A turnout motor installed on a mounting plate screwed to the underside of the baseboard. An extended operating pin passes through a hole in the baseboard and locates in the hole in the tie-bar holding the point blades together. This changes the direction of the points.

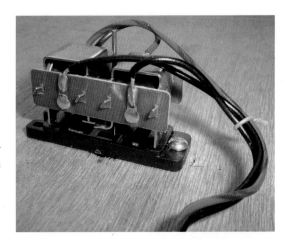

Below: Push-button (also called push-to-make) switches in use on a small control panel for changing the points. An example of a passing contact switch is also shown. These are manufactured specifically for controlling point motors and are designed so that the supply literally passes either of the two contacts but does not remain connected to them.

visually intrusive, and on the scenic sections of a layout something a bit less obvious is desirable. Point motors are also available for mounting underneath the baseboard, minimising their visual impact. Whilst they can be installed directly underneath a turnout, fitting into the slots in some of the sleepers at the end of the point blades, this requires a large hole to be cut in the baseboard for the motor to fit in. It is easier, I believe, to use the point motors with extended operating pins mounted under the baseboard. These are attached to a mounting plate which is in turn screwed to the underside of the baseboard with a hole drilled beneath the tie-bar for each motor.

The instructions provided with the point motors are generally easy to follow. A 16V AC supply should be used – most controllers, as mentioned above, incorporate suitable outputs. One side of each solenoid should be linked by means of a short loop of wire (at the rear in the photograph above) to one terminal of the power supply.

A common return can be run right around the layout connecting the return sides of all the point motors together – there is no need for individual wires back to the power supply from each point motor. The other side of each solenoid is individually connected to the other power supply terminal via a switch. When the switch is operated and current flows through the solenoid the point changes.

Push-button switches are ideal for turnout operation. They should be pushed for just long enough for the point to change. An alternative is a 'passing contact' switch, which is manufactured specifically for this application. An example of one of these in use is shown below, held in place by its own mounting plate. It is critical that, whatever type of switch is used, it only supplies a short burst of electricity to the solenoids and does not allow the supply to remain connected to them.

When point motors are being added to a crossover or a single or double slip two point motors will be required, one for each end of the trackwork. For single slips and crossovers these can be wired together so that one switch works both motors and hence both halves of the trackwork, limiting the scope for setting one set of points the wrong way, which is likely to lead to a derailment. The wiring required to achieve this is shown in the figure below. Two point motors are also required for a double slip, but the operation of the two sets of switches should remain independent to enable the slips to function correctly, and either motor should be treated as a separate turnout.

There are some other types of point motor available, which use an actual motor and

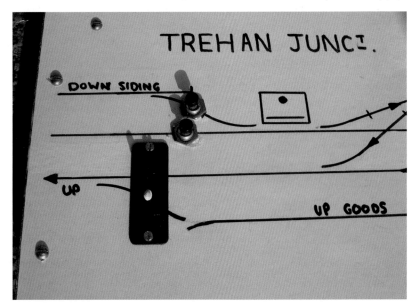

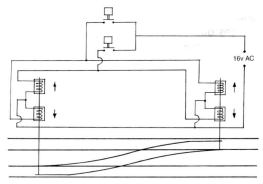

Above: Wiring point motors for a crossover using one set of switches for both parts of the trackwork. If the points work in the opposite directions after installing this wiring, simply reverse the two wires on the 'live' side of one point motor.

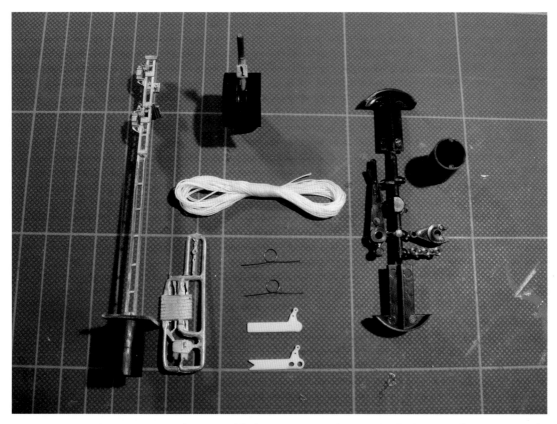

gearing arrangement to move the point blades, rather like the real thing. These are good but quite expensive. If you do want to use them they are supplied with full instructions.

Signals

Signals are a crucial part of the operation of any railway. Although they may seem insignificant on a model layout, it is surprising how obvious their absence can be, and a basic system takes little effort to install.

In my opinion the logic and skill behind signalling is an aspect of railway modelling that becomes all the more fascinating the more you discover about it. A flick through some of the books on the subject outlined in the 'Recommended Reading' list will demonstrate the huge variation in signals that existed, with numerous combinations of arms, posts, bracket arrangements and so forth. Southern Railway signals, for example, were unusual in that, as an economy measure, the signal posts were almost always constructed from two old rails bolted together. Great Western signals, perpetuated on BR's Western Region, were unusual in that they always lowered to an approximately 45° angle to denote 'all clear', whereas in later years most other railway companies adopted signals which were *raised* to about 45° to indicate a clear line ahead.

Signals on which the arm falls to an 'off' position are called 'lower-quadrant' signals, whereas those on which the arm rises to indicate a clear line ahead are 'upper-quadrant' signals.

As the name suggests, a 'stop' signal tells the driver of train when he must stop or when it is safe to proceed along the next section of track, rather like the green and red lights on a road traffic light. Distant signals provide advance warning that the next stop signal is at danger. They are unlike a traffic light in that they are located a considerable distance (often 1,000yd or more) before the stop signal to which they relate, allowing a heavy train to slow down and be ready to come to a halt at the stop signal.

For modellers there are a few pre-fabricated signals available, but these are very generic and cover only a limited range of signal-arm combinations. However, there are a large number of signal kits reflecting the variety of signals found alongside the railways of Great Britain, and these allow realistic models of the signals of specific railway companies to be constructed fairly easily. The figures overleaf demonstrate various stages in the construction of a kit of a Southern Railway version of a signal combining a 'stop' signal and a 'distant' on a common signal post.

Signal kits are usually supplied with levers to operate the signals. The 'distant' lever shown in

Left: The majority of the items within a signal kit. The signal arms can be seen at the bottom of the picture. The distant signal arm has had the holes for the coloured glass 'spectacle plates' drilled out. One of the two lenses will line up with the light produced by the signal lamp for each of the two arm positions so that an appropriately coloured light will be displayed. A green light denotes 'all clear', a yellow light 'caution' and a red light 'stop'. The signal post has been partially assemble, the white-metal components being superglued together. Just to the right of the foot of the post are a few more components awaiting cutting from their sprues and fixing in place.

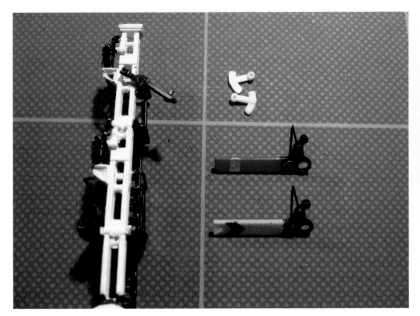

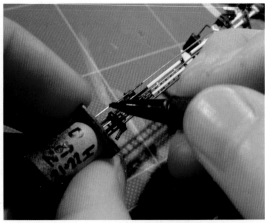

Above: A good way of colouring moving parts black without gumming up the whole works with paint is to use a permanent marker pen. Here one is being used to colour the operating wires of the signal.

Above: The business end of the signal almost finished. Details on the signal post which would have been painted black have been picked out with matt-black oil paint, and the signal arms painted the correct colours. A pin has been inserted in the arms to act as a pivot which passes through a hole (not readily apparent in this photograph) in the signal post.

the picture on the previous page has been painted yellow to match the signal and is shown complete. The 'home' lever is shown as supplied – it is very easy to assemble. The signal and the lever will eventually be connected by the cord shown, and the springs visible just above the signal arms will be used to return the signal to 'danger'.

Once a signal post has been assembled, a very effective way of painting all the little nooks and crannies is to spray the whole signal post, with all the moving parts removed. A car spray paint such as a white primer is ideal. When using spray paint it is much better to build up a colour by applying a few thin coats rather a single thick coat; this avoids obliterating detail such as bolt heads or getting unsightly drips

running down the post. For this signal four thin coats of white paint were required.

The small crank-like objects shown in the figure above left are called backlight blinders and work in conjunction with a small light projected backwards from the signal lamp (the backlight). When the signal is 'on' or horizontal a small white light is visible to the rear of the signal, and this tells the signalman that the signal lamp is alight; if oil signal lamps are in use it tells him that the lamp has not run out of oil. When the signal is 'off' or clear the blinder rotates with the signal arm pivot and blocks this light so that the small white light to the rear of the signal is hidden. This informs the signalman that the signal has responded to his lever at night when the arm

Left: Drilling out the spectacle plates in the signal arms and filling them with coloured see-through 'glass' is a modification well worth making if it has not already been done as part of the kit. The easiest way to install 'glass' in the spectacle holes is to use a product such as 'Liquid Glass', which is shown here. This is run around the inside of the hole, and a thin film is then teased across the hole with the tip of a screwdriver or cocktail stick. It is like PVA glue in that, although it starts white, it dries clear and can then be given a coat of see-through paint such as that sold for use with stained glass. Inspection of a prototypical signal will reveal that what would be expected to be a green glass is often more blue in shade; this is because an oil-burning signal lamp would give off quite a yellowish light which, when combined with blue-tinted glass, would provide a green light to the driver.

Left: The finished signal installed on the layout, in a perhaps less than absolutely vertical fashion. This gives a far more detailed representation of a Southern Railway signal than could be achieved with an off-the-shelf variety, which goes a long way towards creating a sense of region and period around a model railway.

Below: The kind of signal which would require construction from scratch, in this case a Great Western example. *A. Attewell*

Left: A Great Western version of the same arrangement of signal arms modelled above, showing the detailed variation that existed between the different railway companies' approaches to solving the same problem. This signal includes an electric motor to operate the distant (the dark-grey square and circular box at the front of the post at the top of the darker-painted section). Also of interest are the relay cabinet (to the left of the post) and the Automatic Train Control ramp, which can just be seen between the rails. A kit of this type of signal is also available and can be constructed using the techniques described opposite. *A. Attewell*

Right: A short 'O'-gauge distant signal, for the 7mm:ft-scale layout Yes Tor Junction, in the process of construction from scratch. An etched brass arm is installed on a wooden post with a cast white-metal finial, signal lamp and balance weight. Parts of the balance-weight mechanism are also cast brass.

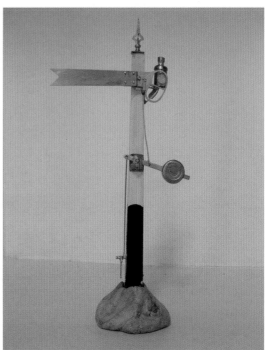

itself is invisible, so he knows that the signal wire has not broken. In model form backlight blinders are 'superglued' to the end of the pivot pin through the signal arm to keep the arm in place. They were usually provided only on signals facing away from the signalbox, but it is useful to fit them on all model signals.

Once constructing signals from kits has been mastered, you can begin to experiment by merging parts from different kits to create custom-made signals. However, in the interests of absolute accuracy it is sometimes necessary to construct signals more or less from scratch. This is not particularly difficult (except in small scales such as 2mm, when everything becomes a bit more fiddly), and a good range of component parts is available to ease the process.

Frequently the parts produced are either etched or cast metal. An ability to work with these materials is therefore necessary if you are aiming to construct unusual signals from scratch. A bit of practice at soldering (as explained in earlier chapters) and the construction of white-metal kits (as explained above) are the principal skills required.

Colour-light signals

A glance about a few railway stations today will demonstrate that, in the majority of locations, signalling has moved beyond the graceful semaphores described above. It was discovered that these required a significant degree of skilled maintenance, which is, of course, costly. In many places they now have been replaced with what at first glance appear rather like traffic lights, albeit with a slightly more confusing array of lights.

Left: The finished signal installed on Yes Tor Junction. The signal needed to be relatively short, as it had to be visible under this small and as yet unpainted road bridge. The vertical stripe on the rear of the distant signal may appear unusual, but is in fact historically accurate. Distant signal arms were originally red with a vertical white stripe on the front and vertical black stripe on the rear. The London & South Western Railway changed the stripe on the front to the familiar chevron *c*1910, but it was not until 1927, when the front of the arms was changed to yellow, that the stripe on the rear became a chevron to match the front.

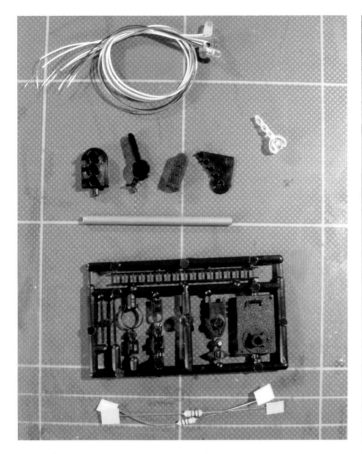

Above: An off-the-shelf colour-light signal from 'Traintronics', showing two amber aspects (yellow to all but railwaymen), usually referred to as 'double amber'. Whereas red, yellow and green lights meant exactly the same on colour-light signals as they had on semaphores, double amber was an extra refinement made possible by the introduction of four-aspect signals such as that shown here. A double-amber aspect means that the next signal will be displaying a single amber, and the one after that a red, its purpose being to give advance warning to a driver that he will be required to stop.

Above left: The component parts of a colour-light kit, in this case for a three-aspect signal with a route indicator (or 'feathers'). The model route indicator is made up from the second, fourth and fifth elements from the left of the top row of components. In reality it is a row of five white lights which light up when a particular turnout in front of the signal is set for a diverging route.

Left: The finished signal installed on the layout. A single-amber aspect from a yellow LED can just about be discerned in the bright sunlight of a summer's day. This means that the driver should expect the next signal to be red.

Colour-light signals are likely to be far more appropriate on a modern model railway than their semaphore predecessors. Fortunately, a number of good ready-built models of these signals are available. The same is true of kits, which allow signals to be constructed for some of the awkward locations not covered by the range of pre-constructed signals.

To fit situations not covered by the kits it is possible to build from scratch, although there is less variety amongst colour-light signals, and the ready-made and kit-built units available will tend to fit far more situations than will the equivalent semaphores. Usually you will need to construct only part of a colour-light signal to suit a particular location. For example, it may be necessary to support a signal gantry from scratch to span a number of tracks, although the signal heads themselves can be used from a kit.

If you do need to build your own signal heads (perhaps if you are modelling in a scale other than 4mm:ft) there are a wide variety of miniature bulbs available. Small filament bulbs, such as grain-of-wheat or grain-of-rice bulbs, are quite bright and can be coloured with translucent paint. Light-emitting diodes (LEDs) can also be used; these emit slightly less light but do not get hot in operation and are now included in most signal kits.

Plastic is a suitable material for construction of LED-based signals but tends to melt if brighter filament bulbs are used. These usually require the construction of metal signals to withstand the extra heat generated.

Signal operation

The location and layout of railway signals is explained well in a number of the books listed in the 'Recommended Reading' section and thus will not be described in detail here. Instead I have concentrated on outlining the ways in which signals can be controlled once installed on a model railway.

Signals can be operated in similar ways to turnouts, i.e. either by hand, by mechanical control or by electrical control. Hand control works best with ready-made signals, as the counterweight is usually large enough to allow easy finger operation.

Mechanical control can be arranged in a similar way to that used to control points. If Ratio signal kits are used, a very similar system of cord-and-spring control is supplied with them.

Like turnout control, it is difficult to carry mechanical control systems for model signals across baseboard joints. If you want all the controls for the points and signals on your layout to be grouped together in one place, akin to a signalbox, but the signals are spread out across several baseboards, then electrical control will be required for some signals. This can be achieved in a number of ways. Point motors can be used, of either the motorised or the solenoid type. In the case of the latter it is best to mount them horizontally and use a crank to drive the signal; otherwise the weight of the steel part of the point motor will always pull it in one direction. If a normal solenoid point motor is used it should be controlled as above with either push-button switches or a passing contact switch to ensure that the coil is not energised for more than a second or two.

It is also possible to use a different type of solenoid which can be permanently turned on to pull the steel armature in one direction against a spring. It is usually best to install this type horizontally, with a crank to change the horizontal movement to vertical movement. The solenoid is controlled with a simple on/off switch supplying 12V DC. When energised the solenoid magnetically pulls a piece of steel into its centre, pulling the signal 'off'. When the current is turned off, the spring pulls the piece of steel back out of the solenoid and restores the arm to 'danger'.

Electrical control is, of course, required for colour-light signals. In the case of a two-aspect signal a simple on/on supply can be arranged by means of a changeover switch. Three-aspect

Right: A pair of signal levers and a point lever, grouped together for ease of operation. The signal levers are supplied with Ratio signal kits and are easy to put together. A common colour coding was used by virtually all English railway companies for point and signal levers: black for points, red for stop signals and yellow for distants. Some other colours were also used: white was spare, blue denoted a locking mechanism for a facing point, and brown was associated with level crossings.

signals require slightly more involved control so that the correct aspect (yellow or green) is displayed. Two- and three-aspect signals should be wired as shown in the diagram on the right.

Route indicators can be controlled by a switch mounted on the bottom of a point motor, if the point to which the route indicator applies is electrically operated. A simple 12V circuit is used, although the feathers should usually not appear if the signal is at 'danger'. A second set of contacts on the switch for the signal should be used to supply electricity only to the point-motor switch (and hence the bulb illuminating the route indicator) if the signal is 'off'. Eckon signal kits with route indicators are supplied with two resistors. One needs to be fitted between the route indicator's negative wire and the negative supply, and the other between the negative wires of the colour lights and the negative supply. I am the wrong kind of engineer to be able to explain exactly why this is (I suspect it must be something to do with voltage bias) but if you do not use the two resistors the signal will not work!

If you find all the talk of signal control (especially the electrical part) a little daunting, do not be disheartened. There is absolutely no requirement for a model railway to have perfectly operating signals; they represent but one facet of railway modelling, to which attention can be turned once construction has been completed, or even years in the future, once experience and knowledge have been gained. In this case you have only to refer to the 'Recommended Reading' section mentioned above, wherein you will find listed a number of excellent books on the subject. However, if signalling is definitely not for you, read on, for the following chapters contain much else that is likely to be of interest.

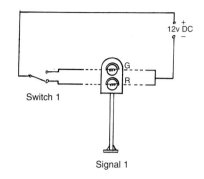

Signal 1

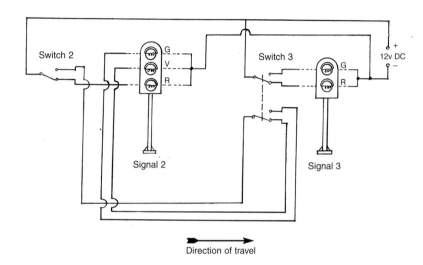

Direction of travel

Above: Control of colour-light signals. If LEDs (rather than the alternative of small filament bulbs) are used in a model signal it is almost always necessary to use a resistor to limit the voltage applied to each LED. A double-pole double-throw switch will be required for the control of Signal 3 on this diagram, so that both sets of contacts change at once.

8 Structures

Below: A fine study of a Great Western wooden post signal and a fairly standard platform, with paving slabs at the edges and a gravelled surface down the middle. This is South Brent, the junction for the Kingsbridge branch, on the south side of Dartmoor, in 1957.
A. Attewell

The railways of Great Britain were in general heftily engineered affairs, constructed when things were built to last and when building things was, relatively speaking, much cheaper than it is today. Thus there are around the country some impressive and imposing structures which carry railway lines over deep river valleys or through steep hills. There are also numerous less-imposing structures, such as small retaining walls supporting a house perched high above a railway line or little brick-built culverts carrying the track over a stream. Such structures are an integral part of the railway scene in this country, and it is important that an appropriate proportion of them be incorporated on a model railway if it is to look believable. This chapter discusses ways in which they can be modelled.

Platforms

The majority of model railways are based around a station, so a platform is a structure that virtually all of them incorporate. There are a variety of ways in which platforms can be constructed, although all should ideally be constructed using substantially the same method, or the layout will look slightly confused.

Significant variation exists in the types of platform in use on the prototype. Early platforms were usually surfaced only around station buildings, the rest of the platform surface being ash or stone. Platforms were then often paved over, and today tarmac surfaces are more common. The height of platforms has also increased over time. During the 19th century they were usually around 2ft higher than rail level, but this height rose gradually through the 20th century, and the modern standard is 3ft. Lines of brick or stone can be seen along the top of many platforms where thin layers have been added. The construction of the platform wall also varies from place to place, often making use of whatever building material was available locally. Timber platforms were sometimes built out over embankments or across bridges to reduce weight, and the Southern Railway produced its own range of pre-cast concrete platforms which could be installed anywhere on its network. The platforms used on a model railway should be

Below: The timber platform at Caradoc Falls, a small country halt on the line from Aberystwyth to Carmarthen.

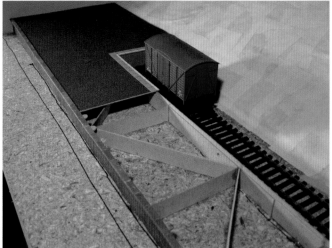

Above: Cardboard-kit platforms at Casterbridge. These were very easy to cut to the desired shape, taking a few hours to put together for the whole layout. The platform on the left is supported on the small wooden blocks visible to the rear. Eventually the landscape will be made up to platform level, and the blocks will disappear from view.

Above: Here a plastic platform wall has been used on the left and a cardboard platform kit to construct the right-hand wall and to provide the platform surface. Individual coping stones moulded into the plastic wall have been coloured with acrylic paint. The bracing beneath the platform surface holds the walls vertical and provides extra support for the former.

correct for the area being re-created. A model of a Southern Railway station would be greatly enhanced by a representation of a Southern pre-cast concrete platform, but such a structure would look somewhat out of place on a layout set in Scotland!

The easiest way to construct a platform is to use pre-fabricated units which slot together. The only problem with this approach is that the geometry of the available units tends to dictate that of the model railway, which is a bit of a 'tail-wagging-the-dog' situation. In many cases the pre-fabricated platforms will also not quite provide the shape you require. This is particularly true if you wish to incorporate a bay or a gently curved platform. In such cases it is necessary to use one of the platform kits available, which can loosely be categorised as those made from cardboard and those from plastic. The cardboard versions generally include everything required to construct a complete platform, whereas when constructing platforms from plastic the walls and platform surface are often bought as individual components.

The cardboard kits are particularly easy to assemble and can be cut to any shape required for a specific track layout. All that is generally required to assemble these kits is a cutting knife and some UHU or Bostik glue.

When establishing the profile for a curved platform face it is important to consider the 'centre throw' and 'end throw' of the longest

coach the layout is likely to see. As coaches usually have some of their wheels some distance from their ends, these ends hang out further beyond the outside of a curve than might be expected, so if the platform has not been installed with this in mind there is a risk that the coach will crash into it. Also, as coaches tend to be relatively long between bogie pivot points their straight sides tend to cut the corner on the inside of a curve, and this too can prove a trap for the unwary. The best way to ensure that these factors have been considered is to mark a paper template on the baseboard and then use this to cut the platform to the required shape. A pencil held against the end and middle of one of the longest coaches used on the layout will allow the required shape to be established. If a reverse curve is installed next to a platform face both

Below: Marking a template to the required shape for a platform edge on the inside of a curve. Centre throw is the most important thing to consider on the inside of a curve, and the pencil should be held against the middle of the coach to establish how great this is.
End throw is more important on the outside of a curve and requires the pencil to be held against the end of the coach.

Above: A large brickwork retaining wall, typical of so many station approaches in larger towns and cities. The poster-boards to the right would make an interesting detail on a model, bringing some relief to an otherwise bland expanse of brickwork.

centre and end throw should be checked adjacent to the reverse in the direction of the curve, and the platform cut to the more restrictive profile of the two.

Retaining walls

Railway lines need to be level across the track (with the exception of a small degree of superelevation around corners). As they are constructed across an undulating landscape it is frequently necessary to cut a shelf into the side of a hill, along which the track can be laid. If sufficient space is available on either side of

the line, cuttings and embankments can be formed to create a level shelf in the natural slope of the landscape. However, in towns and cities where land prices are high the purchase of large tracts for cuttings and embankments is not always a cost-effective way of building a railway, and in such cases it is much more practical and economical to construct a retaining wall beside the railway line in order to raise the ground to the required level.

Model railways often include retaining walls, as they frequently represent busy stations in towns, which provide a greater degree of operational interest. There are a few retaining-wall kits available, such as that shown here, although there are fewer than you might expect. However, do not be deterred, for they can easily be built from scratch.

Retaining walls were constructed from a wide variety of materials and in the detail of their design can differ significantly along a relatively short stretch of line. If these features are faithfully modelled, what could otherwise be a fairly bland expanse of brickwork can be made into an interesting feature.

If building a retaining wall from scratch it is best to design the model by examining a prototype wall of about the same height. You will notice that almost all old retaining walls slope backwards into the ground they are retaining. This is a feature which should definitely be copied to ensure that your wall looks right.

Right: The contents of the Wills retaining-wall kit. Pre-cut materials sheets are provided along with details such as the capping stones for the top of the wall. The infill to the arch can be either brickwork, as used here, or a doorway into a storeroom beneath the railway arches.

There are a number of materials which can be used in construction, among the most effective being cardboard covered in printed brick or stone paper or embossed plastic sheets. The last are slightly more difficult to use if a wide expanse of stonework or brickwork is needed, as they are produced in relatively small sheets and may require a large number of joints, although these can be masked by piers and decorative horizontal lines of brickwork protruding from the main wall. If printed paper or thin materials sheets are used to form the cosmetic covering, a superstructure made up of something slightly more robust will be required. Cardboard from cereal packets is ideal and can be easily glued together using UHU or a similar clear adhesive. Plasticard about 1mm thick can also be used to build the superstructure and will provide a very strong wall.

Above: Constructing the retaining wall behind Gorran's engine shed. The weighty piece of rail with added cardboard supports is being used as a jig to ensure that all the individual pieces of the wall lean into the hillside at the same angle.

Left: The completed retaining wall.

Bridges

In Great Britain there can be few stretches of line over a mile long that do not have a bridge somewhere along their length. Many of the roads in this country (particularly the country lanes and older 'A' and 'B' roads) were already old when the railways appeared on the scene, so numerous bridges were required in order that the roads could pass over the railways (by means of a railway underbridge) or that the new railway lines could pass over the existing roads (a railway overbridge). Bridges were also built to cross rivers and canals, to cross other railways and to enable footpaths to cross the line. Small bridges or culverts were provided to cross streams and cattle creeps, and occupation bridges were sometimes built where the new railway line severed the connection between two fields. I strongly believe that every model railway should include at least one bridge, as they are so prevalent on the

Right: Railway-bridge terminology.

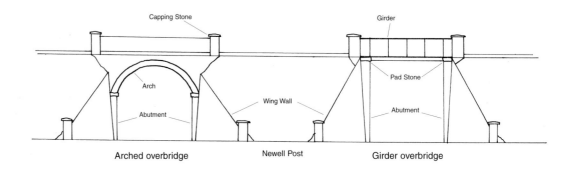

Capping Stone

Arch

Abutment

Wing Wall

Newell Post

Arched overbridge

Girder

Pad Stone

Abutment

Girder overbridge

Above: A Class 08 shunter crosses a long girder overbridge with a train of open wagons. Note the sheet piling around the foot of the embankment – an interesting feature that could easily be modelled. *Author's collection*

Above: Three bridges for the price of one! This is actually not an untypical concentration of bridges for a stretch of railway line in Great Britain. Here a girder underbridge is followed by a light lattice footbridge and a three-arched brick underbridge. For some variation on a model the footbridge could be changed to a pipebridge carrying a water main, gas main or sewer across the railway line. The photograph was taken at Bloxham, Oxfordshire, in 1963. *A. Attewell*

railways of this country. They are also interesting features in their own right, providing something to look at between passing trains.

The most common types of bridge used in this country were arched bridges, in brick or stone, and metal girder bridges. There were, of course, other types, notably the Cambrian Railways' timber trestles, but these were much rarer. Brick or stone arches were preferred by railway companies, as bricks and bricklayers were relatively cheap when most of Britain's railways were built, whereas metal girders had to be fabricated off-site and were thus more expensive. However, if insufficient height was available for a brick arch a metal girder bridge would be used to cross a road or river in order to maintain the right of way beneath it.

Whilst overbridges have been built in a wide variety of ways by railway companies, the design of an overbridge is driven by the fact that it must support the weight of a railway line. Thus some types of bridge were found to be particularly effective and economical, and these were used fairly universally.

With the exception of footbridges, which tend to be fairly light structures and are often constructed from a metal lattice, railway underbridges are usually either arch or girder bridges. The latter were generally only used where height for an arch was limited or for longer spans, where girders start to become more economical than arches. As a rule, generously engineered underbridges were provided by the railway companies for roads crossing a railway line, and such bridges were often similar in design to those provided to carry the weight of a railway line across an overbridge.

When it comes to bridge construction, generalisation within the categories of arch and girder is dangerous and can only be made in a loose sense. Although the arch bridge would appear to be fairly universal, most bridges are actually bespoke to a particular location. For example, many are not quite square to the railway line but at a slight angle to fit into the alignment of the original road. There is also no real reason why the roadway over an arched bridge needs to be level and, where the original

road was on a gradient, the road over the new bridge also tended to follow the old gradient.

It is easiest by far to build a bridge square to the track and with the roadway flat, using one of the kits available. However, if you fancy a bit more of a challenge I encourage you to introduce into your models some of the diversity that can be observed on the prototype. Bridges built at a slight angle or on a gentle gradient do look more realistic and are certainly a talking point. In many cases a kit can be used as a starting point for this kind of bridge and can then be altered to fit a particular situation.

If a straightforward arch bridge is the order of the day, there are a number of good kits and, indeed, pre-fabricated bridges that can be used; I have used parts of various Wills kits to construct the underbridge at the end of the platforms at Gorran. Assembly of these kits is similar to that of a plastic building kit.

A number of variations on the girder-bridge theme were produced by Britain's railway companies, according to the span of the bridge. If a single-track lane was being crossed, small girders could be used below track level. If, however, the span was longer (for example if the

Right: An example of a model bridge built at an angle to the railway line (not immediately apparent here) and to follow the original gradient of the road. The bridge has also been constructed to split above the abutments so that the arch can be removed; this reduces the storage depth required for the board.

Left: Elements from a range of Wills kits being assembled for the bridge over the end of the platforms at Gorran. The wall on the right is the beginning of the retaining wall behind the locomotive shed. In the foreground can be seen parts from the Wills girder-bridge kits, which have been used to make the girders for the double-track spans. The single-track bridge over the locomotive spur is a straightforward underbridge kit, and the piers for the double-track spans have been constructed from scratch using Wills brickwork sheets.

Below: The completed structure in place on the layout.

Left: The bridge in the course of construction. Kits similar to that shown opposite have been used, along with a few extra sheets of brickwork cut out to the required sizes in order to construct parts of the abutments and wing walls of the bridge. I have built this model in place on the layout, rather than building it on the bench as I did with the model buildings. This is a better approach when constructing something around the shape of the landscape.

Below: A meeting of former adversaries on the finished bridge. The ex-Great Western locomotive is in surprisingly good condition for early BR days and may be due a trip to the weathering workshop!

Above: A ballast-decked bridge on the Kingsbridge branch. This is the easiest version of girder bridge to model and is the variety replicated by the author at Gorran. *A. Attewell*

Below: The other option, known by railwaymen as a 'wheel timber' bridge. The longitudinal baulks of wood beneath the rails are known as wheel timbers and rest directly on the beams of the bridge. Transoms (cross-timbers) keep the wheel timbers the correct distance apart, and metal tie-bars keep the whole together. *A. Attewell*

bridge was crossing a double-track railway line or a river), deeper girders were required. These were often placed either side of the track with the bottom of the girder slightly below track level and the top of the girder a few feet above. Various suppliers produce either ready-made girders or kits which can be used to create this kind of bridge. The abutments can be built from one of the kits available or made up from card or plasticard.

If a girder bridge is being constructed a gap in the trackbase will probably be required for it. This is due to the fact that the deck of a girder bridge is much thinner than that of an arch; a trackbase can usually be disguised within the structural depth of an arched bridge, eliminating the need for a gap.

The overbridge for the lane at the end of the yard at Gorran has a small span, and elements from two of the single-track Wills underbridge kits have been used. The abutments for one track are stone, as supplied with the kits, but for some variation and to add character to the model those beneath the second track are constructed from brick-embossed plastic sheet. There are around the country many examples of similar bridges which have at some point been extended in a manner different from that employed at the time of their construction. The change in abutment material has been included to suggest that the line was built as a single-track branch and later doubled. By adding little carefully thought-through details like this to a model railway, which an interested onlooker can ponder between trains, a whole history can be created around a fictitious layout.

Track was carried over girder bridges in one of two ways. Either a flat deck was provided between girders, which was covered in ballast on which the track was then laid, or the track was carried on special longitudinal timbers ('wheel timbers') which rested directly on the beams of the bridge. The former method is by far the easier to model, but with a little careful work the sleepers can be trimmed away to replicate the latter system; however, some sleepers should be left so as to represent the transoms or cross-timbers between girders and to ensure that the model track remains true to gauge.

Left: Moorswater, Cornwall, 1957. This photograph, taken in the opposite direction from that reproduced in Chapter 2, features the stone-arch viaduct built in 1881 to replace Brunel's timber trestle version. The piers of the latter still stand today and can clearly be seen between the arches on the right. *A. Attewell*

Viaducts

Viaducts are, in effect, extended bridges, used when the gap to be crossed is too great for a single bridge. In their most common form they consist of a number of arches set on piers, with abutments at either end to hold back the embankment. These instantly recognisable arched railway viaducts stride across some extremely picturesque valleys, notably Monsal Dale in the Peak District and the wide valley crossed by the Ribblehead Viaduct in the Pennines, and it is not surprising that many modellers should like to include the graceful outline of a railway viaduct within their model landscape.

When constructing a viaduct most modellers use one of the plastic or cardboard kits available. Plastic kits are no more difficult to assemble than their cardboard counterparts and can be more robust, particularly for taller viaducts. If something more unusual is desired the timber trestle viaducts synonymous with Brunel's lines in the West Country offer an alternative, albeit one likely to require building from scratch. Lofty iron lattice bridges, as found at Crumlin in South Wales and Belah Moor in the Pennines, can also offer unusual alternatives to the familiar arched structure.

I have assembled a cardboard kit of a relatively low viaduct for inclusion on Gorran. It is rather like a shortened version of the viaduct found crossing the Itchen Valley at Shawford on the old Didcot, Newbury & Southampton route, before it joined the Southern Railway main line to Southampton. Assembling a cardboard kit like this is a similar process to that explained in Chapter 9 with regard to the construction of cardboard buildings. The majority of the parts are pre-cut, needing only a few small cuts with a Stanley knife to release them from the surrounding sheet. The whole structure can be glued together with a clear all-purpose adhesive such as UHU or Bostik. It took me an afternoon to put together this four-arch double-track viaduct kit, at the end of which I glued the completed model into place on the layout. The speed of construction and the fact that no lengthy painting process is necessary are, to my mind, distinct advantages that cardboard kits hold over their plastic counterparts.

Below: Some of the components of a cardboard red-brick-viaduct kit. A grey cardboard structure is provided (some parts of this are shown on the right) which gives a solid central core around which the printed cardboard sheets are then glued.

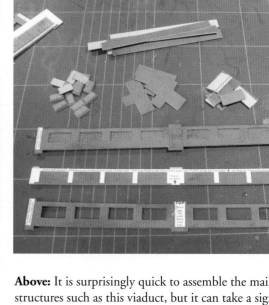

Above: It is surprisingly quick to assemble the main units of structures such as this viaduct, but it can take a significant length of time to add all the little details, like the parapet walls, and for speed and efficiency the author batch-produces items. All of the two-part capping stones required have been cut out of the various sheets on which they were supplied and stuck together (as seen above the left-hand end of the parapet wall) so that they can all be installed in a single operation once the parapet walling is added to the model.

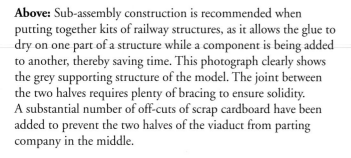

Above: Sub-assembly construction is recommended when putting together kits of railway structures, as it allows the glue to dry on one part of a structure while a component is being added to another, thereby saving time. This photograph clearly shows the grey supporting structure of the model. The joint between the two halves requires plenty of bracing to ensure solidity. A substantial number of off-cuts of scrap cardboard have been added to prevent the two halves of the viaduct from parting company in the middle.

Right: Gluing the final finishing strips of capping stones to the top of the viaduct's wing walls. With small or thin components such as this it is often easier to add glue to the small item before fixing it to the model rather than to dab glue on the model, which can end up with the glue running down the face of the model.

Tunnels

From the modeller's perspective tunnels are essentially bridges with a greater distance between each end. It is fairly rare for a model railway to incorporate both ends of a tunnel, as they are used mainly to disguise the end of the scenic section and carry the tracks into the storage sidings. Whole tunnels are available, which can be placed over the track, but these are really for the train set, with improbably steep hillsides which would look out of place on an otherwise accurate model railway. By contrast

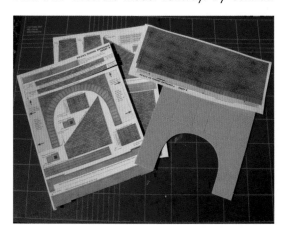

plastic tunnel mouths with 'wing walls' can be painted and installed on the layout to look very convincing. Kits are also available which are easy to make up and allow a degree of alteration. I have used a cardboard kit for the tunnel at the end of Gorran.

The most important feature when constructing a convincing tunnel is not the tunnel mouth but the hillside around it. Despite being substantial structures the mouths of real railway tunnels generally get utterly lost in the vastness of a hillside; indeed, if the hill were not large the railway company would simply have constructed a cutting rather than a tunnel. It is usually impossible to construct a scale model of an open expanse of hillside, because even in a small (2mm or 4mm:ft) scale the hillside would still be huge, and few of us have the space for such a layout. A compromise is, therefore, required.

The appearance of a tunnel can be significantly improved by ensuring that the hillside continues above it, to make visually

Left: The contents of a cardboard tunnel-mouth kit, as used to construct the one at the end of Gorran.

Above: A model of a wrought-iron viaduct based on that at Meldon, on the Southern Railway line around Dartmoor. This has been constructed entirely from plasticard and is extremely robust, due to the fact that the structure is faithfully copied from the carefully designed original. Well over a hundred hours were spent on its construction, and a little over £100-worth of plasticard employed, along with a substantial quantity of gunmetal paint, applied by spray gun rather than by brush.

Right: A Great Western impostor (presumably a diverted service during weekend engineering work) exits the tunnel at Gorran.

obvious the fact that a cutting would not have been an alternative. An easy ruse to avoid losing a considerable length of usable layout is to incorporate a big bushy hedge some distance above the tunnel mouth and curtail the layout just beyond it; this gives the impression that the hillside continues beyond the hedgeline. If space permits, it is also possible to arrange any curves required to connect the scenic section of a layout to the storage sidings beneath the hillside, as shown in Chapter 2 the plan of the layout based on Baker Street. This allows a good section of the hillside above a tunnel to be modelled and avoids the slightly too convenient appearance of a tunnel mouth right at the edge of a layout.

The inside of a tunnel should also be modelled. A simple wrapper of cardboard bent to the appropriate shape and lined with thin brick-embossed plasticard painted a sooty colour is all that is required. It is important that the inside of a tunnel look dark if it is to be convincing. With a little thought it is often possible to box in some of the storage sidings beyond the layout to help create a dank, dark and realistic appearance to the tunnel.

Right: A tunnel nestling amongst the lush vegetation of the Exe Valley. Note that the interior of the tunnel is pitch-dark – model tunnels look ridiculous if you can see daylight and the fiddle yard through them. Also of interest is the low signal-arm position, arranged to ensure that drivers have the best possible view of the signal. *A. Attewell*

Buildings 9

Left: A typical railway building – in this case the goods shed at Watlington, Oxfordshire, in 1957, the year the branch closed to passengers. *A. Attewell*

Railway buildings constitute an integral part of the railway scene. To the railway enthusiast 'ES', 'GS' and 'SB' are instantly recognisable on a plan as an engine shed, a goods shed and a signalbox, and that enthusiast is likely to have in mind a clear image of how these buildings should look. A convincing model railway, therefore, needs convincing model buildings.

Most model railways will incorporate a few (or perhaps a large number) of the buildings commonly found 'beyond the company fence': the houses, pubs and garages which make up the towns and villages served by the railway. Without these there would be no railways, and domestic and industrial buildings can be useful corner-fillers on a model railway. In this chapter

Left: Buildings at a typical railway station, in this case Heyford, Oxfordshire, in 1963. The signalbox and station building are obvious on the near platform, as is a waiting room on the other side of the line. Also evident are a typical smattering of railway huts, huge numbers of which could be found dotted around the railways of Great Britain. *A. Attewell*

Above: The unusual locomotive shed at Tetbury, complete with a water tank across the end. Notice how the track just in front of the shed has been almost obliterated by a combination of ash and coal dust; adding details such as these to a model railway will make it look much more like the real thing.
A. Attewell

When it comes to buildings, the transition from train set to model railway is not that great. I used to have a number of model buildings in my cupboard full of railway things, and every time I got out my train set and took over the living room I would place them in appropriate locations, creating a landscape around the track. My first model railway used exactly the same buildings, and, for ease of storage (to reduce the thickness of the boards), they were not even glued in place and therefore changed location quite frequently.

Assuming sufficient storage space is available, it is desirable to fix buildings to a model railway so that they can then be located in exactly the right position; this is particularly advantageous with the likes of engine sheds and goods sheds, which need to be positioned correctly in relation to the track. If stuck down, buildings can also be blended into the landscape, with greenery added (along with details such as tools leaning against a wall), to make the landscape more believable.

There are a variety of manufacturers, styles and materials available to the model-railway builder. A number of companies now manufacture complete, ready-painted buildings which can be added to your model without further ado. One such is the signalbox in the figure on the right, which has had but a nameplate added to it before being glued to the layout and blended into the scene with a small amount of ivy growing up the wall.

I have concentrated on modelling railway buildings, but the techniques can be applied to any building required for a layout.

Deciding how the urban landscape around a railway line should be arranged is best done, as are most things when it comes to railway modelling, by examining the prototype. This can be achieved either by looking through old maps and books of aerial photographs or, for a modern model railway, by looking through satellite images online.

Right: An option if space is at a premium: half-depth buildings, often termed 'low relief' buildings, can be effective space-savers at the rear of a layout.

Left: A straight-from-the-box signalbox ready for installation. These ready-made models are a quick and easy way to add some buildings to a layout.

Below: The pre-fabricated and pre-painted signalbox installed on Gorran.

The only downside to creating a model railway using pre-constructed buildings is that they make it very difficult to create a feeling of individuality, and it is quite probable that amongst your friends or at exhibitions you will come across other railways using exactly the same buildings. They are also deliberately manufactured to be similar to the style of lots of railway companies but identical to none. This, of course, makes them appeal to a wider audience, but it does make it very difficult to model a particular railway company in a convincing way.

An alternative to using pre-constructed buildings is to make your own, using the many excellent and varied kits available.

Cardboard kits

A number of manufacturers produce ready-printed cardboard kits which are easy and enjoyable to put together. A certain degree of individuality can be introduced during assembly by splicing two kits together or leaving a few bits out of a particular model. As they are ready-printed they are also very quick to make, requiring only cutting out and glueing together to produce the finished article. No lengthy painting process is involved.

Many of the buildings that went with my old train set were cardboard kits, as they make surprisingly strong structures. Some of the steps

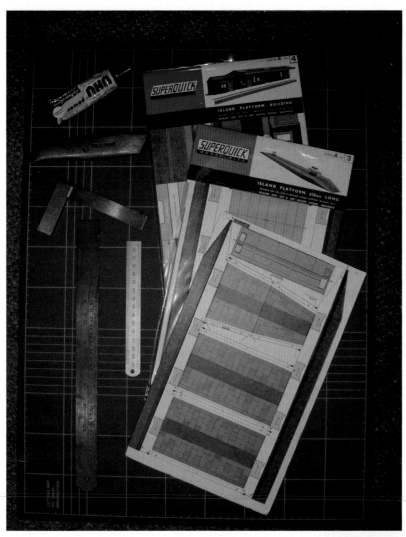

and techniques required to assemble this type of building are demonstrated in the figures below.

In my experience the instructions which come with cardboard kits are comprehensive and easy to follow. The only thing which must be ensured is that the building goes together 'square'. If it does not, some of the pre-cut elements are unlikely to fit in place. The use of a square will help to ensure that everything remains nicely where it is supposed to be.

I must admit that sometimes I do jump ahead of the instructions and have a few different elements of construction on the go at once, rather than doing it all in order, as this saves time which would be spent waiting for glue to dry.

Sometimes the instructions in cardboard kits call for thin strips of only a few millimetres along the edge of a larger piece of card to be bent back on themselves and glued to the back of the larger piece of card in a double thickness. An example of such a situation occurred along the edge of the platform visible in the final figure of this section. It can be quite difficult to get these to stick in the required place, as they tend to lift up along the score line if it is not deep enough. A useful trick in this case is simply to cut off this strip and stick it on as a separate piece of card. A heavy weight can be useful to ensure the joint fits together well. I have a variety of short lengths of narrow-gauge rail, picked up over the years as paperweights in various railway shops, which are ideal for this purpose.

Above: Cardboard buildings, platforms and bridges can be constructed using the simple tools shown here: a ruler, a modelling knife (with a sharp blade to ensure precision), a square and some glue. For this station the author used two island-platform kits and spliced them together for extra length, discarding the ramp ends from one.

Right: Using a square to make sure a building goes together as intended. The lines on the cutting mat can also be used to ensure squareness, although this is more difficult.

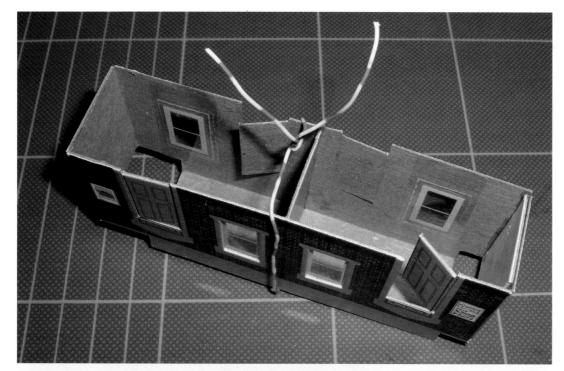

Left: A simple clamp which will eliminate the need to hold something together whilst the glue dries (in this case the glue holding the central partition in the building). It is simply a length of single-core electrical wire cut from telephone or network cable, wrapped around the relevant section of building and twisted together to the appropriate tightness. Do not be tempted to make it too tight, as the wire will eventually cut into the cardboard and distort the shape of the building.

Left: A variety of sub-assemblies under simultaneous construction, to reduce waiting-for-the-glue-to-stick time. The piece of rail on the left is keeping a door in place on the rear of the staff-room wall while it sticks. One side of the awning (in the background) is being held together with little twists of wire, while the second waiting room (right) is about to receive some attention.

Plastic kits

A large number of plastic building kits are available. These are quite easy to put together, requiring little more skill than is needed for a cardboard kit. The range of buildings that can be bought as plastic kits is relatively broad, enabling more appropriate models to be constructed for a particular layout than the range of cardboard kits would perhaps allow.

Often, different kits are available for different railway companies. Kits can be purchased for some quite specific buildings, such as the Great Western's pagoda shelters, as used for village halts, or the Southern Railway's concrete gang huts, which were found dotted around its stations. Being easily able to model structures such as these is a definite asset to modellers, enabling them to create a real sense of period and place.

Right: The Midland Railway signalbox at Settle Junction, the start of the famous Settle-Carlisle route. This signalbox is still painted in Midland Railway colours to this day, so a model MR-style 'box would be essential for any layout purporting to represent this classic location. *Author's collection*

The following figure shows the contents of a typical plastic kit, in this case a water tower, which forms part of Ratio's Locomotive Servicing Depot kit. Included are number of plastic 'sprues' (frames) holding a number of components of the kit itself. A few basic tools are required to assemble plastic kits: a sharp modelling knife is essential, a ruler is useful in some cases, a reasonably sized file (a 4in second cut is ideal) to smooth straight edges can be useful, and, of course, a tube of plastic glue is required. Also shown in the photograph is a smaller flat file, one of a set of needle files that can be used to fettle parts to a snug fit. A good set of instructions is usually provided with a plastic kit, often including an exploded drawing of the finished model. This can be particularly useful for explaining where all the little details should go.

As I do with cardboard kits, I usually start by constructing a number of sub-assemblies, as I find it easier to add detail to smaller sections which can be more easily handled before the

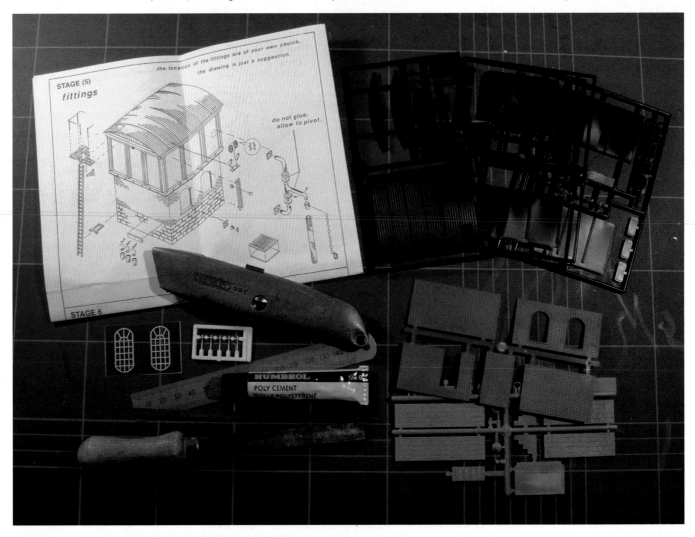

The contents of a plastic kit of a water tower, along with the tools required to assemble it. The plastic components are on the right, held together on their sprues awaiting liberation with the modelling knife. Sometimes a small amount of filing is required to remove the remains of the connection between model and sprue. This particular kit includes pre-printed windows, which are a very useful addition; they will be the last items to be added to the model, once all the painting has been done.

whole is glued together. As plastic kits tend to be well designed and accurately produced they generally go together quite quickly. The main structural sub-assemblies usually consist of four or so walls or a few parts of a roof, and before long these can be stacked on top of one another to check how the building will look, which provides a satisfying feeling of progress. Details can be added if appropriate; it was at this stage that I added the door and door furniture to the brick base of the water tower. However, some details, such as the ladder up the side of the water tower, have to wait until later in the assembly process.

Sometimes a few alterations can be made to plastic kits; for example another window let into a wall or a window bricked up with the addition of a bit of brick-embossed plastic to the rear of the wall. This helps to add individuality to a kit building. In the case of the water tower I gave the corrugated-iron roof some attention with a coarse file, thinning down the edges to give it the ragged, rusted look that corrugated iron develops over time.

It is by no means necessary to add an interior to all model buildings, but in some cases a few internal details can significantly enhance a model. One such building at Gorran was the feed store constructed for the goods yard. As the doors were modelled slightly open, the interior would be visible. The walls were therefore given a whitewash, and the floor a quick coat of brown paint to make it look like wooden flooring. Pre-cast concrete stores such as this were usually used by agricultural feed merchants for selling their products. The interior could therefore be expected to contain sacks of feed ready for distribution to local farms. As the doors are not wide open I felt the need to model only one pallet of sacks, in front of the doorway.

Another improvement which can be made to the buildings for a model railway is the addition of internal lighting. This is particularly worthwhile if time has been spent adding interior detail to a model building. 'Grain of wheat' bulbs (small filament bulbs) can be used for this purpose, although these give out quite a bit of heat, so it is important to ensure that they are not mounted directly adjacent to a flammable wall. LEDs tend to give a harsher, bluish-white light, which is probably appropriate for modern buildings lit by fluorescent tubes but less so for older, gas- or oil-lit structures. To enhance the impression of oil lighting, 12V 'grain of wheat' bulbs can be operated from a 6V or 9V battery, giving a more yellowish light.

Above: Gluing together the stonework base of the water tower A square is being used to ensure a neat corner. Polystyrene cement is the adhesive here, being smeared along one surface of the joint before the two parts are brought together. This is probably the easiest-to-use and least-hazardous plastic glue available, but it does take quite a long time to set.

Below: The alternative to polystyrene cement. This is a liquid solvent-type glue, which is applied to a joint using a brush (as shown) while the joint is held together by gentle pressure. The solvent melts a little of the plastic on either side of the joint, and the two surfaces then join as one. This glue can be harmful if misused and is not suitable for children. However, it does make a much quicker (almost instantaneous) bond between plastic components, which is advantageous to adult modellers wishing to make progress. I often use a wooden block to hold the glue bottle to prevent it from getting knocked over. Boring out a piece of 2x2 timber to the appropriate size and adding a large flat base is well worth the effort – you definitely do *not* want to spill this stuff everywhere!

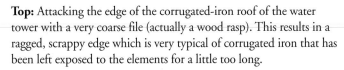

Top: Attacking the edge of the corrugated-iron roof of the water tower with a very coarse file (actually a wood rasp). This results in a ragged, scrappy edge which is very typical of corrugated iron that has been left exposed to the elements for a little too long.

Above: The completed sub-assemblies, ready for gluing together and detailing. Some details, such as the door in the brick base, have already been added, as have two splice pieces (attached to the stone base) to strengthen the bond between components.

Right: The interior of the locomotive shed at Cardigan. It appears bare at first, but there are many small details here which could enhance a model. The bench just inside the door, for example, could be included, complete with its sizeable vice for running repairs to engines, and a casting of a bottle jack could be picked up at an exhibition and leant against the wall. A hose has been provided in the ash pit, and a spare section, together with a bucket, appears to be hanging on the wall. *A. Attewell*

Above: The completed kit, with all sub-assemblies glued together and the chosen details added. The kit is actually supplied with more items, such as fire buckets, but the author has saved these for use elsewhere. The plastic lamp-bracket has also been replaced by a piece of brass wire, for robustness.

Partial kits and scratch-building

Despite the plethora of kits on sale it may be that none is suitable for a particular model railway, which might require an especially characterful building, as constructed by the early railway companies, or an odd-shaped structure, such as a station building between a high-level overbridge and the platforms below. In such circumstances a certain amount of scratch-building may be required.

Partial kits straddle the boundary between plastic kits and scratch-building and offer an extremely good starting point for honing scratch-building skills. There is a good variety of partial kits available in Wills' 'Craftsman' range. These include comprehensive instructions, a selection of sheets of brick- and slate- embossed material and also mouldings of tricky details such as window frames and chimney pots.

Individual walls or roof sections are usually not pre-moulded in partial kits; instead sheet material is provided, along with drawings and templates for cutting and assembling. This provides the opportunity for the building to be

Above left: An interior detail carefully placed to enhance a model feed store. Although, in reality, the sacks would probably have been stacked in the corner of the building they would be almost invisible if modelled in this location.

Above: The feed store installed on the layout. The partially open doors will be noted, as will the sacks within, upon sufficiently close scrutiny under better light!

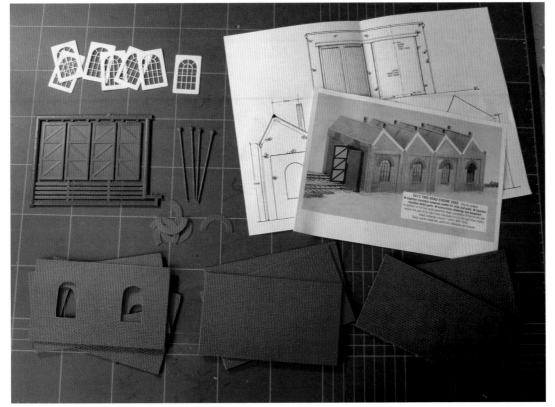

Left: The majority of the contents of the engine-shed kit from the Wills 'Craftsman' range. Sheets of brick- and slate-embossed material are provided, together with sheets including pre-cut window holes and mouldings of doors and guttering.

techniques required go beyond the scope of this book but are covered in the books listed in the 'Recommended Reading' section.

Painting

Unlike pre-printed cardboard kits, plastic kits and scratch-built models will require painting before they can be installed on the layout. This is not difficult, and the painting instructions provided in kits today are much better than those of the past. Metal items, such as water pipes and guttering, and wooden items, such as the pretty valances around platform canopies, can easily be painted the correct colour using oil paints. Particular railway colours, for example Great Western Stone No 1, are available pre-mixed from manufacturers like Railmatch and Precision. Acrylic paints are generally easier to mix than oil paints and can be thinned down by using water rather than turpentine.

To ensure that the finished model has a realistic finish it is best to use matt or satin paints. Gloss tends to be unrealistically shiny when used on models as, in reality, it would quickly lose its shine when exposed to the weather. If, however, gloss is the only paint available in the correct colour the finish can be toned down by blowing talcum powder at the model while the paint is wet; this disrupts the smooth, reflective surface of the gloss paint and gives the finished model a 'flatter' appearance akin to that of buildings that have spent a few winters being ravaged by the

Above: These kits are also suitable for sub-assembly construction, as the walls are more easily fabricated as individual units which can then be glued together to form the finished building. Creating the walls as complete sub-assemblies before forming them into a building has two advantages: firstly, the corners are much easier to glue together when multiple thicknesses of plastic sheet are laminated together at corner pillars; secondly, final assembly of the building is satisfyingly swift if the laborious detailing has all been completed beforehand!

Right: Buildings constructed from scratch at Yes Tor Junction. These have been assembled around a thin plywood core with stone-embossed plastic glued to the surface and painted. Details such as the cut stone quoins and lintels are almost all created from plasticard.

altered during construction to the design required. In this instance I have replaced the doors in one end wall with a brick-built wall made from additional brick-embossed sheets purchased separately from a model shop, which are more appropriate for the eventual location of the building.

Scratch-building can often involve significant investment of time and effort, but great satisfaction can be derived from designing and constructing buildings which meet perfectly the requirements of your model railway. The

elements. By making sure that they are finished in matt colours – or adding a thin wash of brown paint to the finished article, to create the impression of grubbiness – models can be made to look far more realistic. These 'weathering' techniques are described throughout this book and in more detail in some of those listed in the 'Recommended Reading' section.

The first step when painting stonework is to apply a mortar colour as a background. I tend to use a tan or sand-coloured paint, although a touch of grey or white can be added, depending upon the mortar colour desired. It is usually best to thin the paint to the approximate consistency of single cream to ensure that it gets well into all the gaps representing the mortar joints and to stop it filling up the mortar courses (which it will do if it is too thick). When thinned with water the paint will be less likely to adhere to the plastic, as it tends to form droplets on the surface, but as long as it is worked into the mortar courses this does not really matter, as the bricks and stones will be repainted later.

The next step starts with squeezing some brown (burnt umber) and mid-grey paint onto a palette or scrap piece of plasticard or the top of a plastic pot and mixing together a small quantity of each until a suitable stonework colour is achieved. A number of stones, picked out at random across the whole structure, are then painted in this colour until the paint on the brush runs out. A little more of one colour or the other is then added to the mix as a way of subtly altering the shade, and a few more stones are picked out at random. This procedure is repeated until the stonework is fully painted.

When moulded plastic brickwork, such as the Wills materials sheets, is being painted, the same tan or sand-coloured acrylic paint, worked well into the mortar courses, is applied to the whole area of brickwork. Although it would be possible to paint every brick individually, using exactly the same technique as that adopted for stonework, I have to admit I have never been particularly keen to pursue this course of action! It is much easier to exploit the fact that each

brick is raised above the surrounding mortar courses and use the following technique to apply brick-coloured paint to the protruding bricks, leaving untouched the mortar between them. (This is why it is important not to fill up the mortar courses with mortar-coloured paint; if you do so, the bricks will not protrude above the surrounding paint, and it will be impossible to paint them in this way.)

The required technique is often called 'drybrushing' and involves running a fairly dry brush over the surface of the model. Light but firm brushing at a 45° angle to the rows of bricks is best, as this minimises the chance of the bristles'

Above: Cardboard kits and pre-painted buildings can all be improved by a bit of careful re-touching with a paintbrush. The improvement made to a modern pre-painted hut by some careful toning-down of the paint colour and addition of some undergrowth is apparent.

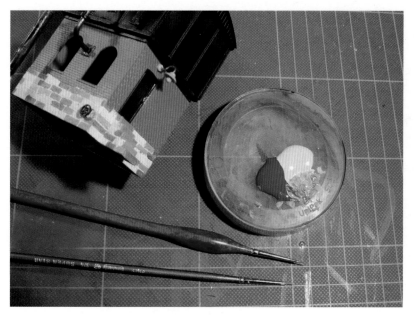

various shades of brick colour, so different amounts of different shades can be mixed together for each charge of the brush, to create variation across a wall.

Corrugated iron is one of my favourite materials to model, as so much subtle dilapidation and decay can be added with a few layers of paint, significantly enhancing the character and believability of a model building. Once painted with a base colour, which can often benefit from matting down with a little talcum powder, the ridges of the corrugated iron can be picked out in a lighter shade of paint, using the dry-brushing technique. This accentuates the darkness of the furrows, where grime tends to accumulate. A rusty colour mixed up from red and brown paint can also be dry-brushed around the edges of the sheet material, which is usually where rust starts to attack the building.

Concrete is another material commonly used around railways, particularly the Southern, where products of the Exmouth Junction concrete factory can be seen in almost every corner. It can, however, be a tricky shade to replicate in paint, as there is a tendency to use too much cream or yellow; in reality concrete is usually mostly grey. When painting a model in a concrete colour, the first step is to apply a base coat of concrete-coloured paint; I usually use an oil paint. Once this is dry I add a thin wash of black acrylic paint, to provide variation across the surface of the concrete and to imitate grime in the corners. As discussed above in relation to the thinned-down tan paint used for mortar, the thin dark wash will often not stick properly when first applied, but if a rag is used to spread it around the concrete panels it will usually stick to the surface of the oil paint. Some further grime can be added with a thin dribble of brown paint in the corners and joints of the structure.

Above: Part-way through the process of painting the stonework base of the water tower. The whole area has been painted in a mortar colour, and roughly half the stones have then been treated, at random, with the various shades the author has mixed up.

getting caught in the mortar courses and painting them by mistake.

When a dry brush is used, ridges or protrusions will tend to pick up paint, whereas dips and furrows will not. To get a 'dry brush' the brush should be charged with a minimal amount of paint. The easiest way is to load the brush with paint of the chosen colour and then to paint most of this out on a piece of paper or the edge of the palette, and only when a very small amount remains on the brush should it be used for dry-brushing across the bricks. Practice is undoubtedly required with this technique, but once mastered it really is a very easy way of painting brickwork.

I find it easier to dry-brush using oil paint rather than acrylics. Oil paint tends to be thicker and is therefore less prone to dripping off the brush and landing somewhere you do not want it. Jars of paint can be purchased pre-mixed to

Right: Stages in painting a brick building, in this case the engine shed. The bay on the far left is unpainted, that second from left has had a thin coat of mortar applied, and those third and fourth from left have had brick-coloured paint dry-brushed across the surface of the wall.

Left: Typical brick-built railway structures, in this case a coal office and weighbridge hut.
Notice how the brickwork of the coal office (in the foreground) changes character halfway along, the mortar lines becoming much clearer; perhaps the original structure was a lean-to affair, abutting a larger building now demolished, or perhaps at some point it was struck by something and had to be rebuilt. Details such as this can easily be added to a model building by careful painting.

Left: Dry-brushing the corrugated-iron roof of the water tower. The actual base colour is gunmetal, toned down with a fair quantity of black. A lighter shade is being mixed for the dry-brushing, although some black is still being added, the mixing being done on the top of an old plastic pot (foreground); most of the colour is then painted out on the edges of the pot before the last remnants of each brushload are lightly wiped across the structure.

Left: Adding some rust (in this case painted directly rather than dry-brushed) to the corners of a corrugated-iron lamp-hut. The desired colour is mixed on the dish from red and brown oil paints to match the rusty key (centre). The bottle at the top of the picture contains oil-paint thinner, a small amount of which is mixed into the paint to make it easier to apply.

Right: The finished water tower. The recommended techniques for painting stone, bricks and corrugated iron have all been used on this model. It is important that model buildings be installed in advance of the ground covering; there is little point in covering a whole yard with mud and cinders and then sticking the building on top of it. Addition of some greenery around the base of the structure can help make the structure look like it is bedded into the landscape.

Right: A Southern Railway concrete gang hut at Horsted Keynes, on the Bluebell Railway. When mixing paint to a specific colour such as concrete, a colour photograph of the real thing is often invaluable. *Author's collection*

Above: The station building at Aberaeron, looking remarkably smart in the early 1960s. Small corrugated-iron extensions such as this can be added to building kits to create some individuality and provide a challenge to the modeller keen to acquire some scratch-building skills. *A. Attewell*

Left: Casterbridge's cardboard-kit-built engine shed and goods shed, the latter assembled in plastic from a Wills 'Craftsman' kit.

Creating the Landscape

Left: Creating a supporting structure for the scenic shell on an open-frame baseboard. I usually employ a straightforward diagonal lattice structure, although the shape is somewhat complicated here by the change in the angle of the slope at the bottom of the embankment and the need to fit around the piers of the viaduct.

When faced with an 8ft x 4ft expanse of baseboard one might be tempted to cover the entire thing in railway line. However, most railways actually travel through the landscape, be it the mountains of the West Highlands, the seemingly endless fields of East Anglia or the steep-sided valleys of South Wales. When choosing a prototype for a model railway many people tend to gravitate towards country branch-line stations rather than vast city marshalling yards or grand main-line termini. This is entirely sensible, considering the amount of space that most of us are allowed to allot to a model railway in our homes. An ability to create a convincing rural scenic landscape in this confined space is, therefore, important to the model-railway builder. This chapter explains many of the techniques required to create a model of the landscape, both within and beyond the company fence.

The scenic shell

Construction of scenery almost always starts with the construction of the ground itself, which I have termed the scenic shell. Although the landscape could be built straight onto an extension of the flat trackbase, scenery built on the flat tends to look unconvincing.

There are a number of ways in which an undulating ground profile can be achieved, and all have their pros and cons. Plaster-impregnated bandage is a material which is frequently used to form a scenic shell, and a number of proprietary products are available. All consist of strips of bandage material with plaster powder trapped within the weave of the fabric. To form the scenic shell these strips of bandage are moistened and smoothed into place over a supporting framework, often made out of chicken wire. The process is straightforward, but the resulting shell can be heavy and brittle, and if a small piece of the landscape is chipped off by accident a bright white gouge in the model suddenly appears. It is possible to improve this situation by adding (to the water used to moisten the plaster) brown poster paint and PVA glue, which introduces ductility to the final scenic shell and takes the edge off the whiteness of the plaster. However, I prefer to use *papier mâché* coated in PVA glue to

Above: Stages in constructing a *papier mâché* landscape on a foundation of foam insulation board. Two layers of insulation board can be seen on the left, and the stages in covering these with *papier mâché* can be seen on the right. The process is described in detail in the text.

form a base for the landscape. This is a very cheap and straightforward method which creates a surprisingly robust surface.

The *papier mâché* needs to be built over a supporting framework. If a flat-topped baseboard has been constructed, foam insulation board is a good, light and cheap way of providing the necessary support. Insulation board can be purchased from most DIY stores, in sheets about 2in thick with a thin foil covering to each surface. Chunks of foam of approximately the size required can be cut from the sheet and glued into position on the baseboard layer upon layer until the required height is reached. The foil surface should be roughened to ensure that the glue sticks to it; the easiest way is to use a knife to cut a criss-cross pattern into the foil. The board has a slight tendency to curl up at the edges whilst being glued in layers; to counteract this, books can be used, as shown in Chapter 4 with regard to gluing down cork flooring tiles. If some slight curling still occurs it can easily be covered over with *papier mâché* at a later stage.

Once the glue has dried, the foam can be carved to form the shape required. A cheap breadknife is a good tool for this. Purchasing one specifically for modelling is recommended, as little pockets of not-quite-dry-yet glue can remain between the layers of foam, which can get stuck to the knife and create a tricky situation out of which to try to explain your way if you've borrowed the knife from the kitchen!

If open-frame baseboards have been used, a network of cardboard strips can be constructed to support the *papier mâché* scenic shell. Cereal packets cut into strips about half an inch wide are ideal, and a glue gun is a good tool for attaching them to the frame of the baseboard.

Once the supporting structure has been constructed, the shell itself can be added. I usually first paint a layer of PVA glue over the supporting structure to ensure that the first layer of newspaper sticks well to the framework. Multiple layers of newspaper are then added, each painted liberally with wallpaper paste with an inch brush; I used about four layers when constructing Gorran. After this a layer of white

Left: Creating the scenic shell. A large number of pieces of newspaper of various sizes have been ripped up ready for use, and a good quantity of wallpaper paste has been mixed. This job is far quicker (and therefore slightly less boring) if you are well prepared!

paper is added on top of the newspaper to make the finished surface easier to paint. Once the wallpaper paste has dried thoroughly (usually a day or two later) a generous coat of PVA glue is painted over the white paper to toughen the shell. Finally the whole landscape is painted brown using acrylic, poster paint or emulsion.

Ground coverings

Once the landscape shell has been constructed and the buildings installed on a layout there is likely to be showing through a reasonable expanse of brown-painted land, which needs covering. There are a range of materials which can be employed to cover the scenic shell and a variety of techniques are used to install them.

When grassland is being modelled it is easiest to use a fabric mat dyed to the correct colour and stuck down onto the landscape shell. Pre-made fabric mats of 'grass' can be purchased and create a very realistic effect, but they can be quite expensive if used over a large area.

An alternative to using bought-in grass mats is to dye material yourself with olive-green fabric dye. For the majority of the grassland on Gorran I have used a thin blanket-like material which was purchased from a fabric shop. Surgical lint can also be used to good effect, as can material sold for teddy-bear fur! If the latter is used it should first be dyed approximately the desired shade of green before being stuck in place on the layout. Variation can be added to an area of grass once stuck down by brushing acrylic paint onto it.

Above: After an initial coat of PVA glue approximately four layers of newspaper are added before a final layer of white paper, necessary to provide a clean surface for painting. This is visible in the background of this photograph.

Left: A very brown landscape at Gorran just after painting. This view also provides a behind-the-scenes shot of the thick cardboard landscape-formers which have been used in places. These are perfectly adequate for the job and help minimise the weight of the board.

Right: Installing a mat of grass-like material in the field just behind the engine shed at Gorran. This is pressed down into a layer of PVA glue and provides very realistic-looking (albeit costly) grass.

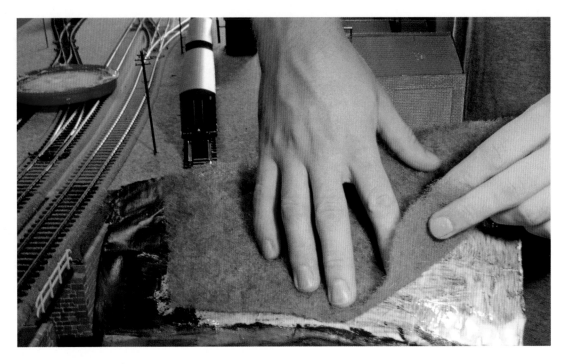

A number of specialist materials enable the modeller to replicate foliage, some of which can be used to enhance model grassland. A range of textures is available, all of which have their specific uses, and these now come in many different colours. Indeed, scenic materials are now available in so many subtly differing shades that having an idea of the season in which a model railway is set is desirable in order to narrow down the options. Once a decision has been reached on this subject it should obviously be adhered to throughout construction of the layout.

The different textures of scenic material available all have their own names, which often differ between manufacturers. 'Flock' is the name usually given to dyed sawdust, which is available in a wide range of colours. Ground foam, available in a range of greens and browns, has slightly more body and better represents weeds and foliage. Fine-ground foam is called 'turf' by some manufacturers, while less finely ground foam is sometimes called 'coarse turf', and it is

this that I consider the most useful and versatile material for landscape modelling material; ideally suited to representing foliage, it can be added to the sides of buildings or structures and used to cover hedges or trees, as well as to introduce variety to broad areas of grassland.

Hedges and fences

Not only do fences and hedges separate the fields and roads of the landscape, but a fence line also runs alongside almost every railway line in the British Isles.

Fences and hedges are both easy to model. Fences, in particular, take little time or effort to create, as pre-formed plastic items can be purchased. Pre-formed hedges are also available and can be added directly to the landscape. However, these tend to be quite regular in shape and are generally not representative of the average field hedge in large portions of the country.

Fortunately, hedges of any size and shape can be easily manufactured. The basic shape can be created in various ways, for example using lichen or rubberised horsehair. I have found the best material to be the humble green kitchen scouring pad, as recommended in Barry Norman's book *Landscape Modelling*, which is invaluable reading for anyone keen to expand their landscape-modelling skills. A large number of individual pieces of scouring pad should be cut from the sheet to the shape of the cross-section of hedge being constructed (it is amazing how much you will get through). The individual hedge-

Right: Turf (on the left), slightly coarser turf (centre) and flock, in this case coloured to represent ballast (right).

Left: Dyed blanket-like material as used at Gorran to create a large area of grassland. The area on the right has had turf and coarse turf added to create some variation in the grassland similar to that found in rough grazing land. An unimproved area of grassland is shown on the left for comparison.

Below: Hedgerow construction underway. The pile of irregularly shaped pieces of kitchen scouring pad is apparent in the foreground, with a selection of blocks of four of these pieces glued together just behind. A section of hedge that has just been glued together and a completed hedge are visible in the background. If the spray glue is added after the ground covering is installed, the base of the hedge migrates across the ground slightly wherever the glue fell, adding a nice touch of realism.

shaped pieces should then be glued together in blocks of four or so and left to dry. These are then installed on the layout by gluing them together to form a hedge line. The resulting hedge frame is then sprayed with glue (such as that sold for mounting photographs), and a mixture of mainly mid-green coarse-ground flock, with some other shades added for variation, can then be applied to represent the leaves.

Bushes and flowers

Railway lines are often surrounded by odd-shaped parcels of rough land. These are frequently the result of the railway companies' having to buy complete fields when they built their lines, even if they did not need that much space for the railway itself. These areas of land tend to end up neglected and covered in bushes and weeds, particularly in more recent times.

Bushes can be easily modelled. The first stage is to find a structure for the bush to provide its shape. Lichen is particularly good for this and can be purchased in packets from model shops. Other materials, such as rubberised horsehair, can be better for less dense bushes. A piece of the chosen material should be cut to the required size and shape for the bush.

Foliage can then be added using the same method as that used for hedges. When constructing bushes, it is easiest to spray the structure of the bush with glue, add the coarse turf and allow the glue to stick before the completed bush is glued in place on the layout. The process of bush production is demonstrated

Above: A few nettles can be found in the goods yard at Gorran. 'Planting' flowers in a small piece of foliage net or similar is a useful way of making sure they stay upright as the glue dries.

The fabrication of model weeds or flowers is similarly straightforward, and the technique used is essentially the same whatever type of plant is being modelled. The first step is to find a stem. A number of different materials can be used for this purpose including bristles from a soft brush or specially manufactured plant stems. A small amount of PVA is applied to the end of the stem and it is then dipped into a mixture of different colours of coarse ground foam. If a flowering plant is being produced the ground foam can be used as a basis for the flowers, and the plant's head can be picked out in an appropriately coloured paint.

Long grass can also be found in many locations around railway lines. This can be replicated by applying PVA to the location where the clump of long grass is required, and plumber's hemp, a material sold in most good builder's merchants, should be inserted into the glue. Once dry this can be trimmed to the appropriate length with a pair of scissors.

well in the photograph of foliage construction for trees, which is explained further on.

Small low-to-the-ground bushes can be represented using a material called foliage net. This consists of a fine net which is covered in coarse turf and can be ripped into small pieces and glued directly in place on the layout. Extensive use of this material has been made during the construction of Gorran.

Trees

Trees can be seen from almost anywhere in England and should therefore be represented on almost any model railway. A variety of pre-fabricated model trees is available; these are becoming increasingly realistic and are a

Right: Long grass made from plumber's hemp is prominent in the foreground of this photograph. This is a very easy material to use, as it requires no colouring.

Left: An area of ground between the feed store and the lane which has essentially been abandoned. A layer of short grass has been installed to provide a base for the area, and bushes, long grass and weeds have then been added to create an impression of neglect.

tempting way of creating woodland. An example of a small stand of trees assembled from items bought straight off the shelf is shown below.

The trouble with ready-made trees is that they are almost always much smaller than a scale representation of the average English tree should be. The average fully grown tree reaches around 100ft, some, such as beeches, topping out at 120ft. This makes a fully grown beech tree 480mm tall in 4mm scale. Trees this tall actually look a bit too big on model railways, but even a three-quarters-grown tree should be around a foot tall on an 'OO' model. If you want to include a tree this size on your model railway the only option is to make it yourself.

The most important thing to do is to find a photograph or a drawing of a real tree and copy it. This will allow you to get the proportions of the tree correct and to ensure that the general shape of your tree is realistic.

Left: Pre-fabricated trees in use on a small layout.

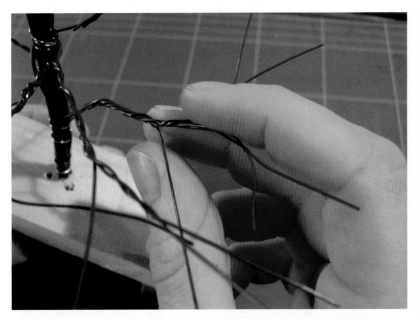

Top: Adding an extra length of tree wire part-way up a tree to form an extra branch.

Top right: The framework of branches for a tree quickly comes together, providing a satisfying feeling of progress.

Above: Using a glue gun to add thickness to the branches and trunk of the tree. A few drops of glue or other irregularities are fine; they simply add character and will hardly be noticeable once the tree is finished. If a section goes really wrong it can simply be pulled off the wire branch and re-done!

Right: The finished tree trunk and branches, ready for some foliage. The relief added by the hot glue can be compared to the previous picture of bare wire.

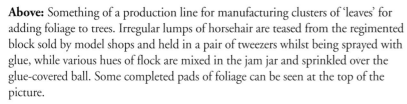

Above: Something of a production line for manufacturing clusters of 'leaves' for adding foliage to trees. Irregular lumps of horsehair are teased from the regimented block sold by model shops and held in a pair of tweezers whilst being sprayed with glue, while various hues of flock are mixed in the jam jar and sprinkled over the glue-covered ball. Some completed pads of foliage can be seen at the top of the picture.

Above: The completed tree ready for installation on a layout.

The first step is to create a wire framework for the branches. Soft iron wire, which must be soft enough to bend by hand, can be purchased from model shops. A bundle of this wire should be secured together with a loop tied around the base, and the individual branches then twisted into shape.

Once the framework has been constructed the bark can be added. Plaster can be used for this but will produce brittle branches which may break off if knocked accidentally. An alternative is to use a glue gun to cover all the branches in hot glue; once dried, the branches and trunk can be painted in a mixture of grey and brown. This method is far more durable than the use of plaster and less likely to suffer unfortunate accidents leading to white gashes appearing in the trunk.

Leaves are most easily represented using the same coarse turf recommended for covering hedges and bushes. This is added to a structure of rubberised horsehair to produce small clusters which are then glued to the ends of the branches.

Roads

The railway modeller will sometimes find himself constructing a roadway running alongside the railway line, over a bridge or perhaps into the station yard. Although any railway enthusiast worth his salt will obviously shun such heathen methods of transport, on account of their role in stealing traffic from the railways, roads are sometimes necessary to complete a realistic railway model.

Construction of a road starts with the base. This can be created either as part of the scenic shell, as a flat area built into the *papier mâché*, or on a separate wooden base, rather like the railway line itself. If a separate base is to be

Below: The layers of card used to create a cross-fall across this road are clearly visible in this view. A piece of card is later cut to the full width of the road and stuck over these, as can be discerned in the foreground.

Right: The finished lane leading under the bridge at the end of the yard at Gorran. Ground foam has been added to the middle of the lane to add some character.

used thin ply, hardboard or even cardboard are suitable materials, as they are light and can be bent to form the ups and downs of the road.

It should be borne in mind that most roads are not flat in cross-section but include a slight crossfall away from the centreline, to allow water to run off. This can be replicated by adding multiple layers of cardboard to the centre of the road before adding a final cardboard base over the full width, bent slightly over the central rise.

Once the road base has been constructed the surface can be added, the material used depending on what type of road is required. Tarmac will probably be appropriate for more recent layouts, whereas a stone finish will work best for models based more than 50 or so years ago. A mud finish is usually applicable for a rough lane or track, whatever the age.

If tarmac is required, the most realistic results can be obtained by using printed tarmac paper or grey paint. Stone-finished tracks can be constructed with model-railway ballast, but it is advisable not to use the same size of ballast as that used for the railway track, as the similarity will be obvious. It is generally better to use a smaller stone for roads. The lane at Gorran, for example, is surfaced in a mixture of 'N'-gauge ballast and dried mud. The appearance of a road surface is much improved if some fine sand or dried mud is also included, as roads were not surfaced in a single size of stone, like railway ballast, but made up of a variety of sizes, which provided a smoother finish.

If a muddy track is required, dried mud can be glued straight onto the road base. If a really rutted and churned-up track is the order of the day a thin layer of plaster can be added to the road base, and track marks and ruts can be carved into it. This can then be covered in dried mud to provide the texture and colour of a road surface.

Water

Streams and rivers are often under-represented in model-railway landscapes. Even short stetches of line in the UK usually incorporate at least one river bridge or culvert, so an ability to replicate water is important for the authenticity of your model railway.

In general water is best represented by one of the specialist products available such as that used here which generally come with good instructions. For small streams and puddles a single coat of gloss varnish applied on a muddy stream bed can create a convincing impression of dampness. Still water, such as a village pond, can be modelled by cutting a piece of clear plastic to the required size and painting the underside black. This gives a surprisingly realistic impression of water and can also be used to good effect in open-topped water tanks.

I find creating a realistic-looking landscape around a model railway a thoroughly enjoyable process. There are some good books which consider this subject in much more detail than has been possible here, and these are listed in the 'Recommended Reading' section.

Above: Using a specialist product to add a surface to the river beneath the viaduct at Gorran. The piece of scrap wood in the foreground has been screwed temporarily to the front of the layout to contain the liquid within the stream bed which crosses it.

Left: A rapid moorland torrent passes under the viaduct on the 7mm-scale model Yes Tor Junction.

Left: Here the impression of water has been created in the ditch (on the far right of the photograph) by the application of gloss varnish to a stream bed. The stream has been culverted under a track which runs underneath the railway line.

11 The Finishing Touches

Great realism can be achieved by adding little details to a model railway, such as a couple of figures leaning on a gate or a gradient post by the side of the line. Some of these details may not be consciously noticed at first glance, but the overall credibility of a model railway will be significantly enhanced by the addition of little touches like the signalman's bicycle leaning against the signalbox wall. Such details can also be added over time, once the major construction phase is complete, and is particularly pleasurable for those who enjoy constructing their model railway as much as operating it.

This chapter briefly explores ways of modelling some of the small details which are typically found around a railway line. There is no need to include them all on your layout, and the features described certainly not constitute an exhaustive list; rather they have been selected to help provide an overview of techniques which, when coupled with the those described elsewhere in this book, should enable the model-railway builder to replicate almost anything.

Buffer-stops

Buffer-stops are an integral part of the railway scene and serve the equally useful function on a model railway of stopping wagons from falling off the end of sidings – as, of course, they do on the real thing!

Buffer-stop kits come in a variety of scales, and in some a choice is available. The most common buffer-stop in use on the railways of this country was probably the rail-built type, an example of which is shown here. However, there were several varieties: old sleepers were sometimes stood on end in a square and packed with earth, and simple baulks of wood attached to a wall were often used at the end of bay platforms or milk docks. At termini hydraulic buffer-stops were sometimes provided which could reduce the damage to train and passengers if the driver applied the brake too late.

Right: Luggage barrows ready for their next turn of duty. A large range of details such as these are available to the model-railway builder, often as castings requiring little work before they are complete and ready for installation on the layout. *A. Attewell*

Left: An earth-and-sleeper type of buffer-stop at the end of a small loading dock. In such situations this type is more suitable than the ubiquitous rail-built type. *A. Attewell*

Right: Buffer-stop kits in component form (foreground), assembled with a painted lamp (right) and after further work with a paintbrush (left).

Left: A buffer-stop at the end of the locomotive siding at Gorran. A little greenery has been added to the base, and a few strands of plumber's hemp used to represent long grass. The first centimetre or so of rail has also been painted a rusty colour.

Generally, buffer-stop kits are very easy to put together and install. The appearance of a buffer-stop can be enhanced by painting the lamp body white with a red lens. A small paint brush (size 000 or so) is required for this task. Some buffer-stops also had white bands painted on the buffer-beam – examination of prototype photographs will show if this is appropriate for your layout.

The rusty rail colour in which buffer-stop kits are usually moulded can be improved by overpainting in the usual mixture of dark-brown and dark-red paint used for painting rusty metal. In reality buffer-stops situated at the end of infrequently used sidings often got buried in ivy, long grass and weeds, so add a touch of greenery to your kit by attaching coarse turf with small dabs of clear-drying glue.

Telegraph poles

Telegraph poles are visible in more or less every picture of a steam locomotive pulling a train through the countryside. They can be simply made and are one of those little features which can add a lot of realism to a model railway.

Telegraph poles were wooden poles which carried strands of uninsulated electrical wire between signalboxes. They also carried signalling wires around stations, for example wires forming circuits to inform the signalman whether or not an out-of-sight signal was showing the correct indication. As most circuits linked the signalbox with other locations around the station, such as individual signals or telephones in buildings like the engine shed, the number of wires carried tended to reduce as the distance from the signalbox increased. Out in open country only a few wires, for the telephone (often two wires per circuit) and block instruments (usually one, two or three per circuit), would be carried.

The poles' spacing varied between regions. On the Western Region the poles were spaced approximately 24 to the mile, which in later years was increased to around 32 to the mile. The latter spacing scales down to one telegraph pole every 660mm in 4mm scale. On a model railway, where most lengths are compressed, it is better to situate the telegraph poles closer together, or they tend to look a bit odd. On Gorran I have situated them approximately 400mm apart, although the spacing has generally been dictated by the location of buildings, signals, viaducts, railway lines and so forth.

Model telegraph poles can be purchased complete and painted, but their dimensions are often dubious. Alternatively they can be modelled from one of the kits available. For some reason all the kits seem to incorporate four cross-arms, each with four insulators. If these are painted and installed as they come out of the box they can look very much like the telegraph poles on everyone else's layout. It is, however, easy to alter them to create a more bespoke

Right: A Great Western 'Manor' at speed, flashing past telegraph poles as it goes. Here five arms of four insulators have been provided — 20 wires in all. *A. Attewell*

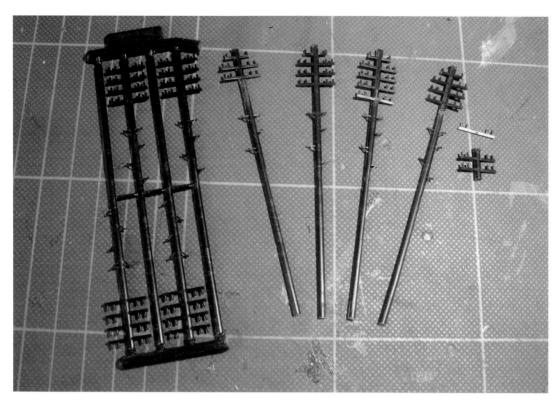

Left: A collection of telegraph poles for Gorran. The poles are supplied as shown on the left. The arms can be cut down, as on the right, to produce poles relevant to a specific location; the pole third from left has been given an extra arm, cut off a spare pole. Individual arms can also be liberated and attached to buildings or signals.

model for a particular situation. For example, some companies frequently had only a pair of insulators on the top cross-rail or -arm. Moreover, a four-arm pole can easily be made into a two- or three-arm pole by simply cutting off an arm or two and filing the resulting surface smooth. Arms thus removed can always be attached later to another pole if desired; if so a small slot will need to be cut into the receiving pole, using a needle file.

The wooden components in telegraph poles can be painted with a mixture of brown, grey and possibly black acrylic. Dry old wood tends to be surprisingly grey in colour. The wires were

Left: Slightly different telegraph poles are visible in this photograph, taken at Cinderford, in the Forest of Dean, in 1964. Arms of varying lengths have been provided to carry nine wires. *A. Attewell*

Right: Heading a passenger train away from Gorran, an 'N'-class Mogul passes the last telegraph pole before the viaduct.

carried on white or red ceramic insulators (red – for danger – for power cables, which were carried on the insulators at the outside of the top arm), and on the model these can be painted with enamel. The real things, incidentally, can often be picked up for a few pounds at exhibitions and make excellent paperweights!

Today most telegraph poles have been replaced by modern insulated multi-core cables which run alongside the railway in concrete troughing. This troughing would also be worth

representing on a modern model railway, using plastic microstrip cut into sections and painted.

Loading-gauges

Loading-gauges were provided by railway companies at the exits from goods yards and were constructed to limit loads to fit the company's standard bridges. They were used to highlight any wagons passing out of the goods yard which were likely to strike a bridge and damage it or the load being carried. This was

Right: A loading gauge at Fowey, Cornwall, as a pannier tank brings a breakdown train from St Blazey into the station. *A. Attewell*

less of a problem with standard railway box vans or brake vans of clearly defined dimensions but could be an issue with open wagons loaded within the yard.

Model loading-gauges can be purchased complete, but, if a more specific model is desired, kits are available to represent the different types produced by the various railway companies. They should be positioned so that they apply to every track on the exit of the yard.

Platform signs

Photographs of railway stations taken in the early years of the 20th century show platforms positively awash with signs. Alongside the smart railway-company signs directing the traveller to adjacent platforms for connecting services, the refreshment room or the stationmaster's office any spare space on buildings or fences seems to have been occupied by enamelled advertisements for tobacco, bicycles or soap. If an authentic model railway from this period is to be constructed it is important that a few of these signs be included.

Station and signalbox nameboards and other railway-company signs can be made up from the range of plastic lettering produced in a variety of sizes by Slaters Plasticard Ltd. The 2mm-high lettering (the smallest available) is ideal for signalbox nameboards in 4mm scale, whilst 3mm-

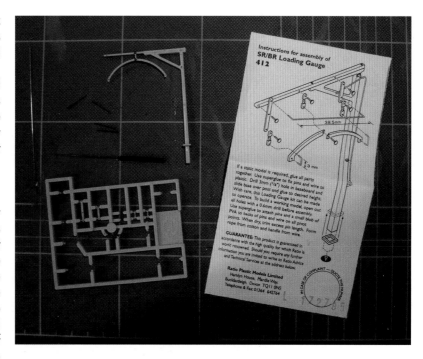

Above: Assembly of a kit of a Southern Railway pre-cast concrete loading-gauge. The plastic components are cut from the sprue and held together by small pins and superglue. If the holes are a little too small to accept the pins provided they can be opened out using a tool called a reamer; these are provided in packs of five or so different sizes and are a useful modelling aid. The author found assembling this kit rather tricky; patience is definitely required, and the superglue should be applied only when the modeller is absolutely satisfied that everything is in the right place!

Left: The completed loading-gauge at the exit to the goods yard at Gorran. The spare sleepers in the foreground have been cut from a scrap piece of track, and, as described previously, some plumber's hemp added to represent long grass.

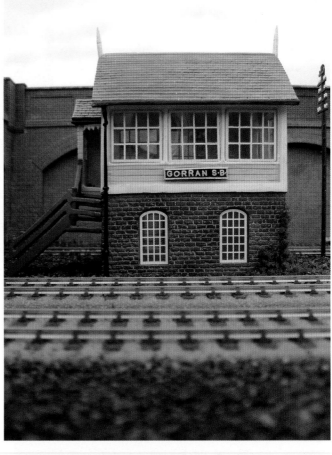

Above: A Great Western station nameboard, along with a bench for the weary traveller. *A. Attewell*

Right: A nameboard installed on the front of the signalbox at Gorran.

Right: Making a sign for the signalbox at Gorran from the 2mm-high range of Slaters lettering. The relevant letters are cut from the sprue and lined up along the ruler. The scriber (shown to the right of the brush) is then used to hold the letters in place whilst the solvent glue is applied with the small brush. Once complete the whole sign can be treated to a thin wash of solvent glue, which evens out any glue marks on the black backing plasticard. Once it is completely dry (usually a day after the glue has been applied) the surface of the sign should be rubbed down gently with fine emery paper to remove any glue and fingerprint marks from the surface of the lettering, thereby providing a nice even finish.

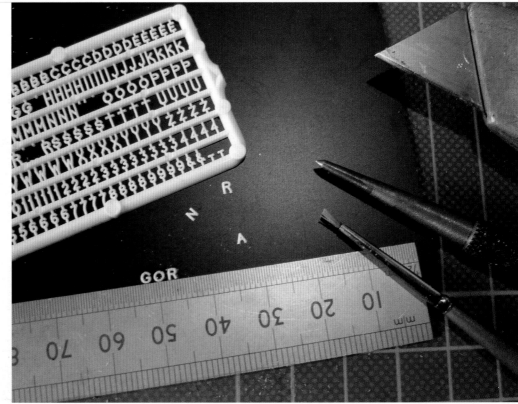

Left: The railways had signs all over the place; this example of another type of sign was photographed at Abingdon, Berkshire (but nowadays in Oxfordshire). *A. Attewell*

Above: Enamelled signs for Gorran. A little reddish-brown paint has been applied to the edges of these signs to create the impression of rust just starting to take hold, and the white paper edges have been blackened with a permanent marker pen.

high lettering works well for station nameboards. The letters are supplied on a sprue and should be cut out individually, using a sharp knife. For signs which will have a black background, I find it easiest to stick the letters to a thin (1/2,000) sheet of black plasticard, which eliminates the need to paint between them at a later date. The letters can be lined up along a ruler and stuck to the backing sheet with solvent glue before a surround is added in 1/2,000 square plasticard strip. Having been left for an hour or so to harden, the completed sign can be cut from the sheet and is ready for installation on the layout.

Printed examples of enamelled signs can be purchased in the more common model-railway scales. All that is required to install them is a bit of careful work with the knife to free them from the paper-backed sheet on which they are provided. The white edges of the sign should also be blackened, either by careful painting or use of a (permanent) marker pen.

The sign can then be installed on the layout using a small drop of UHU glue or similar. Examination of some prototype photographs will reveal the common locations for signs, good places to start being platform fencing and the walls of yard buildings visible to passengers.

People and animals

The key to modelling lifelike figures is to choose your subjects with care. Whilst it may be tempting to add to the edge of the platform a stationmaster vigorously waving a green flag to signal the departure of the train, he will look much less convincing once the train has left. Unlike photographs, model railways are not fixed in time, and figures locked in mid-

Below: A pre-painted figure waiting for the next train.

Right: A few cows beneath the viaduct at Gorran. These are pre-painted animals which have been glued directly in place.

movement poses do not look credible as a train travels past. It is therefore best to represent people sitting down reading a newspaper or leaning against the corner of a building.

The number of figures should also be limited to a sensible number. Photographs of real railway locations (particularly the kind of country branch line that most of us have the space to model) reveal that there were usually few people around. A country station's staff often consisted of a stationmaster, signalman, porter and yard shunter, with perhaps a couple of boys for less-exciting tasks. Passengers too were often thin on the ground at the majority of country locations, particularly in later years.

There are two ways in which a model railway builder can populate a layout. Pre-painted figures can be used, or figures can be purchased as plastic or metal castings and painted by the modeller.

Pre-painted figures represent the simpler, albeit more expensive option. If figures are purchased unpainted the easiest way to paint them is to attach them to strip of plasticard (or a lollipop stick or similar useful handling aid) with a small drop of UHU glue and to paint them slowly, allowing plenty of time for the paint to dry between each coat. Once finished, the figures can be cut free of the stick and then glued in place on the layout with another drop of UHU. The challenge then is to position them in realistic

poses. Reference to photographs can help with this process.

Animals generally move less quickly than people, and choosing a model in a specific pose is therefore generally less important. A mixture of pre-painted animals and unpainted castings is available, depending on the scale of the layout. These should be either glued directly in place or first painted as described above. Reference to photographs (or simply taking a walk through the countryside) is again recommended, to ensure that you model an appropriate number of animals within a given field size and that they are grouped in natural poses.

Road vehicles

For early railways (up to the inter-war years) a horse and cart would be the most appropriate form of road transport that could be included on a layout. Several kits are available to model working horses and a variety of types of cart, and most simply require plastic or white-metal components to be glued together and painted.

There are a number of good ready-made models available in the usual railway scales of a selection of road vehicles from various periods, and these can be added to your layout with a minimal degree of work. However, they can often benefit from a thin wash of brown paint and some subtle weathering to remove their 'straight out of the showroom' shine!

Motor-vehicle kits are also available. These often comprise white-metal or resin components, which are glued together, with a few brass details added, before the complete item is painted. Useful instructions are generally provided with these kits, so their assembly need not be discussed in detail here.

For the lifetime of the majority of railways in Britain private-car ownership was low. Whilst a few examples of cars of the appropriate period can enhance a model railway, do not be tempted to add too many. One reasonably clean and respectable example in the goods yard, perhaps belonging to a local merchant who has come to check some stock, and two or three on the station forecourt are really all that is required. Referring to photographs from the era being represented and replicating only what was actually there on a normal day (rather than what you think would have been there) is the key to creating a credible model railway.

12 Stock

Right: The sort of train which is ideal for the size of railway most of us have room to model. An ex-Great Western Railway pannier tank and a couple of appropriate coaches at Lambourn, near Newbury. The standard of ready-to-run rolling stock available today is so high that stock such as this can be purchased and placed in service on a layout more or less straight out of the box. *A. Attewell*

Until about the turn of the millennium the rolling stock which could be bought pre-painted and ready-to-run was nothing like as good as that which you could construct yourself from scratch. More recently the range and standard of ready-to-run locomotives, carriages and wagons has improved dramatically, and the models available now are extremely accurate; indeed, some are so good that constructing the same items from scratch would be largely a waste of time. Most prolific is the range available in 'OO' gauge, although the choice of models in 'O' and N gauge continues to grow.

Despite the high quality of ready-to-run rolling stocks it is still possible to make small improvements to achieve even more realism. Small details can be added here and there to add individuality to a model, and improbably clean-looking stock can be weathered to give a more dilapidated and aged appearance.

Model trains for model railways

The 'N'-class locomotive featured within these pages is an example of a ready-to-run model which well captured the look and feel of the prototype as soon as it was taken out of its box, but despite this a few improvements have been made to give it a greater feel of individuality.

Real coal, crushed from a lump of anthracite (which has a shinier finish than household coal) has been added to the tender, being spread over the plastic coal already provided with the model. With a bit of careful work with a paint brush, the pipework in the cab has been picked out in copper-coloured paint, and the faces of the pressure gauge and vacuum gauge in white. A model locomotive crew could also be added as a way of further improving the appearance of the cab.

At the front end of the locomotive a pair of Southern Railway headcode discs, cut (using a hole punch) from a sheet of 1/20,000 plasticard, have been added; these informed signalmen as to the type of train being hauled and at night were replaced by lamps in the same positions. The faces of the wheels have also been blackened using a permanent marker pen, care being needed to keep the ink off the wheeltreads, which pick up the electrical current.

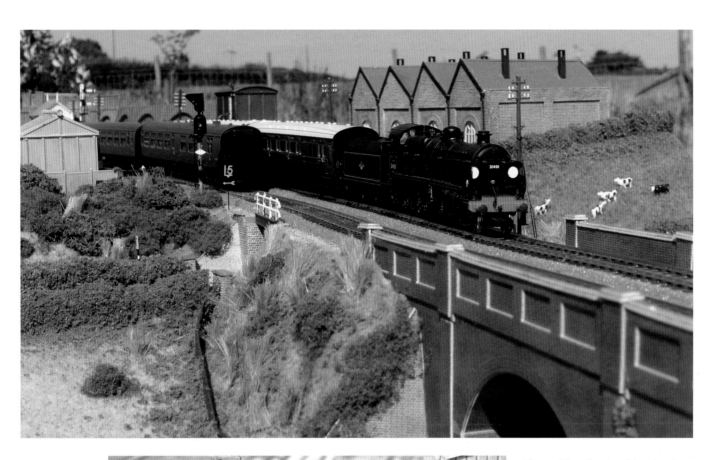

Above: The plasticard headcode discs are prominent in this view of the 'N' heading out over the viaduct.

Left: The 'N'-class Mogul rests between duties in the locomotive siding at Gorran. The real coal in the tender and the painting undertaken in the cab are clearly visible.

Enhancing wagons and coaches

A similar process can be employed to enhance the realism of wagons and coaches. Although weathered rolling stock can now be purchased, it is still sometimes necessary to tone down the finish of an unweathered model. This was the case with the short rake of UK Fertiliser wagons pictured below, which I purchased for another project. In their straight-out-of-the-box condition the paintwork was unrealistically perfect. However, with careful dry-brushing of rust around the underframe and adding some grime to the wagon sides and roof the appearance of these wagons was much improved.

Ready-to-run model coaches can be treated in a very similar fashion if they appear a little too glossy when first taken out of their box. It is, of course, important to ensure that any thin dark washes applied to coach sides do not darken the windows too much!

Building your own stock

Sometimes an item of rolling stock may be required that is seemingly impossible to purchase complete. If the item in question was relatively common on the railway system of this country, it is worth having a browse through the various stock manufacturers' websites to see if the item is planned for future production or is only temporarily unavailable. If it is a more unusual item, the only way of replicating it is probably to build it yourself.

Above: Using the paintbrush seen here the side of this wagon has been treated to a very thin wash of black oil paint; this is then wiped down the side of the wagon with a cotton cloth, which leaves paint in all the corners and makes sure any streaks are vertical and look like they have been created naturally under the influence of gravity and the rain. Some additional dark brown paint has also been dry-brushed around the door furniture of the wagon.

Below: A pair of admittedly somewhat out-of-period UKF wagons in the yard at Gorran. The difference between the subtly weathered vehicle and its shiny, untreated counterpart is readily apparent.

There is a wide range of kits of model engines, coaches and wagons available in all the major model-railway scales.

The assembly of locomotive kits is really beyond the scope of this book. If you require as part the roster at your model engine shed a particular locomotive that can only be constructed from a kit I direct you towards some of the books detailed in the 'Recommended Reading' list.

Wagon and coach kits are usually reasonably straightforward to put together, although the instructions tend to assume that the modeller has some experience of kit assembly and has to hand some good photographs of the prototype. Often the kits are made entirely from plastic mouldings and can be assembled using similar techniques to

those described in Chapter 9 with regard to the construction of model buildings. As with the building kits, wagon kits are most easily put together in small sub-assemblies which are brought together at the end of the process (possibly after painting) to form the finished article.

If you want a specific model of a locomotive, coach or wagon for which no kit is available, it is, of course, possible to build it entirely from scratch. The required elements should be carefully cut from sheets of plasticard or metal – or, indeed, timber or cardboard. There are many good books and magazine articles which describe the scratch-building of various items of rolling stock, some of which, again, are listed in the 'Recommended Reading' section at the end of this book.

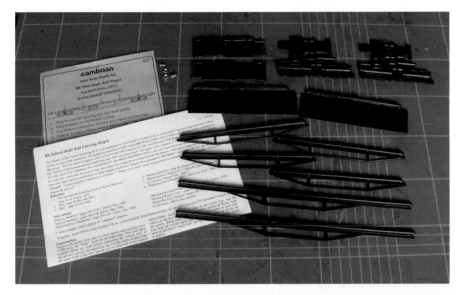

Left: The contents of a kit for a 'Salmon' wagon (a long wagon built for engineering trains to carry 60ft-long track panels without disassembly). The oblong components in the centre form the wagon floor, while the long trusses below these form the underframe, and the components at the top are small detailing items and the bogies. I found some of the items in this kit rather small and fiddly and so chose to omit some. It is admirable that the manufacturers provide all the components required for a truly accurate model, but, when confronted by a particularly fine detail, requiring intricate work, you may consider a model that looks good from 3ft away to be more than adequate for your layout!

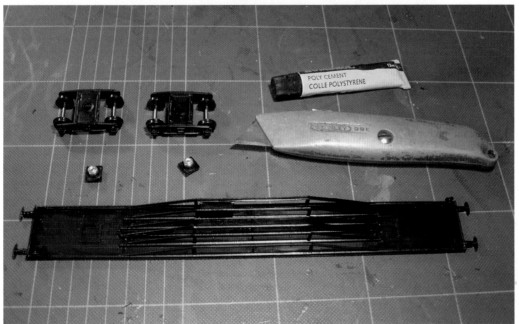

Left: The 'Salmon' wagon was built up as three sub-assemblies, the floor and underframe forming one, and the bogies the other two. The small items below the bogies are the bogie pivots, which were fixed to the underframe. The bogies were hand-painted, and the underframe sprayed matt black, the detail being picked out later in the appropriate colours. Polystyrene cement (as shown here) could be used during wagon-kit assembly, but the author generally prefers a liquid solvent type of glue, as this sets more quickly.

Right: The finished wagon amid a train of engineers' empties, being pulled out of Gorran by a clean and shiny Class 33. This wagon was actually built for another project, which is why it appears out of place on this Southern Railway layout.

Right: A model of a unique London & South Western Railway cattle drovers' van, constructed for Yes Tor Junction. These were built to provide transport for the cattle drovers, who travelled with the livestock carried in the LSWR's fleet of cattle vans; presumably the company considered these men a bit too rough around the edges to be conveyed in even its Third-class coaches!

Living with a Model Railway 13

Left: This picture sums up what owning and running a model railway should all be about. Despite the fact the train has been given the signal to proceed, three men seem to be engaged in replenishing the locomotive's water tanks, and there is a feeling that nothing much is about to happen with any degree of urgency. Those lucky enough to have a permanent home for their model railway can adopt a similarly lazy approach towards running trains, fitting in a few when desired, between the day's other, less enjoyable tasks!
A. Attewell

Once the main construction phase of a model railway has drawn to a close, the way in which it can be enjoyed alters. Rather than spending your days cutting grass to fit an awkwardly shaped field or painting seemingly miles of fencing, you can while away your hours running trains (or admiring your efforts while other people run their trains on your layout). This is not to say, of course, that construction is over for good. If you enjoy constructing a model railway as much as operating it you will always find areas to improve and add detail to. The viaduct and branch line on Yes Tor Junction, for example, originally used to curve in the other direction and have been completely rebuilt, being much improved in the process.

Staging a model railway

Once major construction is complete, a backscene along the back and ends of a layout and a curtain along the front (to hide the supporting legs) can be installed. The visual improvement made by these features is surprisingly significant, as they frame a model railway, disguising the 12in-to-a-foot floor beneath it and the people standing behind it.

A backscene can be most simply constructed from hardboard which is painted blue. This can either be bolted to the rear of the layout or, if it is of significant size, held up on its own supporting structure. Paint sold as 'sky blue' can be a bit *too* blue to look realistic in this situation, and it is often better to mix in a little grey for a closer approximation of the average English sky.

Various companies produce printed backscenes depicting countryside or a townscape. I must admit that I have always been rather doubtful about these, not least because you can end up with your layout dominated by the picture behind it. However, they can certainly be used to create the impression that the landscape continues beyond the confines of your baseboards.

Finally, it is worth painting the front edges of baseboards a nondescript colour to make them less distracting to the eye when viewing the railway. Curtains of a similarly plain colour can also be added beneath the baseboards to hide the baseboard legs and any stock boxes or controllers stored underneath the layout.

Right: Bridge over the lane at the end of the yard at Gorran. If space permits a layout to be erected permanently, rather than stored away when not in use, scenes like this – and the hard work that went into creating them – can be appreciated even when the trains are not running.

Clubs and societies

Railway modelling is much more fun when shared with like-minded people, and to this end I thoroughly recommend seeking out and getting involved with model-railway clubs in your local area.

There are various different kinds of club, and in larger towns and cities you may be lucky enough to have a choice. Some are gauge-specific; the Gauge O Guild, for example, often has local clubs, each with its own test track on which people can run their 'O'-gauge trains. Others are based around construction of a group layout, in which individual members can involved as much or as little as they choose. Some are purely meetings of railway enthusiasts who arrange visits to railway locations and attend lectures about railway subjects.

Right: A blue backdrop behind the viaduct board at the end of Gorran.

Left: Black edges along the front of Gorran. These provide a noticeable improvement to a layout, helping to ensure that the eye does not linger on the baseboard.

A good way to establish the range of clubs in your area is to keep an eye on the exhibition diary printed in railway magazines. Most clubs hold an annual exhibition, which is an ideal opportunity to meet people involved in the local railway-modelling scene. I have always found railway groups to be very welcoming to new members of all interests and abilities. The club secretary is usually the point of contact for people wishing to join a particular group.

Railway clubs cater mainly for people with a general interest in the modelling scene, but there are also a number of societies relating to specific railway companies. If you are constructing a model of a particular line or company I would urge you to seek out an appropriate society and join it. Most subscriptions are very reasonable, and the society in question will provide access to wealth of specialist and often unique information. For example the South Western Circle, covering the erstwhile London & South Western Railway, makes available to its members photographs, drawings and other historical data and also publishes its own quarterly magazine.

Conclusions

I hope that this book has been of use to anyone contemplating the construction of a model railway and that it has explained some of the tasks that may be encountered along the way. However, as stated previously, it is not by any means essential that you should feel confident in all the techniques explained within these pages before embarking upon your chosen project; rather, it is better to start constructing a layout which will, in the greater part, use those techniques with which you are confident and which, once built, will produce the kind of operational challenges you know you will enjoy.

Slowly, new techniques can be tried out around the layout, or perhaps a section of it rebuilt using different methods. In this way your repertoire of modelling skills will increase over time until you have mastered all of the techniques explained herein and you are eager for the next challenge. Once you have reached this stage I would direct you yet again to the 'Recommended Reading' section on page 128, and thence towards the world of scratch-built railway modelling.

Glossary

BRITISH RAILWAYS

AC	Alternating current, whereby the two wires supplying electricity constantly change polarity; mains supply is 240V AC and changes polarity 50 times per second
Ash pit	A pit provided near an engine shed where engines would have their ash plans and smokeboxes cleaned out
Ballast	The angular stone in which railway track is laid, which allows water to drain from the track and can be packed tightly around the track to keep it in place
Barrow crossing	A wooden walkway across the track commonly found at stations to allow luggage barrows to pass from one platform to the other; less common today but very much a feature of pre-Grouping railway stations
Bracket signal	A signal carried out over the track on a bracket to allow it to be seen more easily by approaching trains
British Railways	The name given to the British rail network when nationalised in 1948
Broad gauge	Brunel's original 7ft ¼in gauge for the Great Western Railway
Bullhead rail	The original rail type used by the railways in the country, which was carried in a chair fixed to a sleeper; a progamme to replace it with flat-bottomed rail was initiated after World War 2, but significant stretches remain in use today
Catenary	The name given to overhead electrification equipment
Coaling stage	An elevated stage used to coal locomotives
Conductor rail	The 'third rail' used to supply electricity to electric trains
Culvert	A pipeline or small bridge provided for a stream to pass beneath a railway line
Cutting	A sloping-sided trench cut through the landscape to allow a railway line to be constructed on a (virtually) level plane
DC	Direct current, whereby one wire is always positive and the other always negative
Diamond crossing	The piece of trackwork used to allow two railway lines to cross at an angle
Distant signal	A signal used to provide warning to a driver that he may be required to stop
Double slip	A piece of trackwork consisting of a diamond crossing and four individual pairs of switches to allow greater flexibility between route; often used to save space, as it provides the same function as two separate turnouts but occupies much less space
Embankment	A section of ground which has been deliberately raised to provide a level surface for a railway to be laid
Engine shed	A building provided to house locomotives

Fishplate	The short metal plates used to join rails together (and fixed to them by fishbolts)
Flanges	The vertical part of a wheel which actually keeps the trains on the track
Flat-bottomed rail	A modern rail profile used to replace bullhead rail, being more substantial and thus able to support heavier trains
Gauge	The distance between the inside faces of to railway rails
Goods shed	A building provided to transfer goods from railway wagons into carts or lorries for onward transport
Gradient post	A measure of the slope of a particular section of line; usually expressed as '1 in xxx' , where xxxft is the distance taken to gain (or lose) 1ft in height
Grouping	The process by which the UK's many independent railway companies were combined in 1923 to form the 'Big Four' - the London & North Eastern (LNER), London, Midland & Scottish (LMS), Great Western (GWR) and Southern (SR) railway companies
Home signal	A 'stop' signal used to protect a station from approaching trains
Insulated block joint (IBJ)	A non-conductive joint between two sections of rail, often used for signalling purposes
Level crossing	A crossing provided for a road to cross a railway line, usually including gates to control traffic and trains
Livery	The colour scheme of a particular locomotive or train
Loading dock	A raised platform provided next to a siding to allow easy loading or unloading of goods
Loading-gauge	A gauge provided at the exit from goods yards to ensure that wagons were not loaded in such a way that they would strike bridges
Milk dock	Similar to a loading dock but provided specifically for loading and unloading milk churns
Multiple-aspect signals	Signals comprising lights of more than one colour
Narrow-gauge	Railways built to a gauge narrower than 4ft 8½in
Occupation crossing	Similar to a level crossing but usually only for farm use (*e.g.* between fields)
OHLE	Overhead line equipment - the infrastructure needed to hold a wire above the track to supply electricity to electric trains
Overbridge	A bridge used by the railway to cross something else, such as a river or a lane
Platform	The elevated area provided for passengers to access trains
Point	The piece of trackwork used to join two railway lines into one
Point lever	The lever used to change a point and decide which way a train will go; usually provided only in yards, as on the main line the points are usually controlled from the signalbox
Point motor	A machine for operating points electrically
Point rodding	The rods used to operate points remotely from a signalbox
Pots	The coloquial name given to conductor rail pots which are used to elevate the conductor rail to the required level and insulate it from the sleepers

Pre-Grouping	The period before 1923, when around 25 railway companies were 'grouped' to form the 'Big Four'
Private-owner wagon	A wagon owned by a particular mine or business (such as the Ocean or Emlyn collieries) but running on the national railway network
Relay cabinet	A weatherproof box provided at the lineside to contain signalling relays or equipment
Signalbox	A building provided to house the point and signal controls for a particular location
Signal gantry	A collection of signals for individual tracks mounted on a common bridge above the track
Signal wires	The wires used to operate signals from a signalbox
Single slip	A piece of trackwork which consists of a diamond crossing and two sets of switches
Sleeper	The thick baulks of timber placed transversely at intervals beneath the rails to support them
Speed restriction	A restriction on train speed due to the condition or alignment of the track
Standard gauge	The gauge in most common use in the United Kingdom - 4ft 8½in (or 1,435mm)
Substation	A collection of buildings housing transformers and switchgear used to supply electricity to the third rail or overhead line
Telegraph pole	A pole used to support the individual uninsulated wires used to carry electrical circuits between signalboxes and around stations
Tie-bar	A bar used to hold together the two wheel timbers of a wheel timber bridge; also used to hold the rails together in areas where the sleepers have started to rot but have not yet been replaced
Tramway	A lightly laid railway line usually used for transporting goods or minerals
Transition curve	A curve of increasing radius used to change gently from a straight section of track to a constantly curved section
Turnout	Another name for a set of points
Turntable	A section of track which pivots in the middle and can be used to turn locomotives (in particular tender engines)
Underbridge	A bridge which carries the railway beneath something else such as a lane
Water crane	A water tank surmounted by an elevated hose, used to supply water to steam locomotives; also known as a water column
Water tower	An elevated tank used to store water which can be quickly transferred through a large hose to a steam locomotive
Water troughs	A long trough provided between the rails to allow passing trains to pick up water without stopping
Wheel timber	A large timber used to support the rail on a metal girder bridge
Wheel tread	The flatter section of a railway wheel, which is angled slightly to encourage the train to run correctly on straight track

MODEL RAILWAYS

Analogue control   The traditional system of model railway control which altered the speed of trains by varying the voltage applied to the rails

Baseboard   The wooden supporting structure for a model railway

Cassette   A train storage cradle usually consisting of aluminium angles screwed to a piece of wood; a number of cassettes can be used for each train, and trains can be re-marshalled by swapping around the cassettes

Controller   The electrical component which adjusts the voltage supplied to the track and hence the speed of the trains

Crossing   The part of a turnout or diamond or slip where two rails cross

Digital Command Control   A modern system of train control which is slightly more expensive than analogue control but which involves much less wiring to control multiple trains on one layout

Diorama   A very small layout, often simply constructed to allow trains to be displayed in prototypical surroundings

Fiddle yard   The area used to store trains which are not running on the scenic portion of a layout at a particular time

Fishplate   A folded metal clip used to join sections of track

Flat-topped baseboard   A simple table-like baseboard, particularly good for stations and other flat areas

Frog   A term sometimes used (by manufacturers of model railway track) to describe a crossing

Modern image   A term used to describe models of the post-steam era

Open-frame baseboard   A slightlymore complicated form of baseboard which is particularly appropriate when modelling railway lines running across open country

Prototype   The real, 12in-to-a-foot railway

Ready to run   The name used to describe trains which can simply be taken out of the box and placed on the layout

Relay   An electro-mechanical device which can be used to switch multiple circuits

Scale   The ratio of the dimensions of the real thing to those of the model

Scratch-building   Constructing items such as buildings, trains or track 'from scratch' using basic materials

Transformer   An electrical component used to convert electricity from one voltage to another, usually the 240V DC mains supply to the 16V AC used by controllers and point motors

Traverser   A section of baseboard upon which is laid a number of straight sidings used to store trains and which can be slid at a right-angle to the incoming track to select an individual siding without the need for complex and space-consuming pointwork

Recommended Reading

The table below lists some of the large number of very good books about railway modelling which are available.

Title	Author	Publisher	ISBN	Comments
Peco Setrack HO/OO Plan Book	Peco	Peco Publications	9700000018647	Useful track plans for Setrack-based layouts
Aspects of Modelling: Baseboards for Model Railways	Ian Morton	Ian Allan	9780711031531	
Aspects of Modelling: Digital Command Control	Ian Morton	Ian Allan	9780711031524	
Aspects of Modelling: Road Vehicles for Model Railways	Ian Morton	Ian Allan	9780711031548	
Aspects of Modelling: Track Layouts	Anthony New	Ian Allan	9780711033559	
British Railway Signalling Practice	Peter Kay	Institution of Railway Signal Engineers	9780902390225	
British Railway Stations in Colour for the Modeller and Historian	Nick Jardine	Ian Allan	9781857801231	This series of books forms a very useful reference library for a modeller
Building a Model Railway: Designing a Layout	Barry Norman	Wild Swan	9781874103394	
Cottage Modelling for Pendon	Chris Pilton	Wild Swan	9780906867570	Scratch-building model buildings for the epic fine-scale model railway near Didcot
Creating the Scenic Landscape	Trevor Booth	Silver Link	9781857940237	
Great Western Signalling	A. Vaughan	Oxford Publishing Co	0902888080	
Landscape Modelling	Barry Norman	Wild Swan	0906867444	The essential book for landscape modelling
Layouts for Limited Spaces	Nigel Adams	Silver Link	9781857940558	
Locomotive and Rolling Stock Construction	Trevor Booth	Silver Link	9781857940381	
Model Railway Wiring	Cyril Freezer	Patrick Stephens Ltd	1852601736	
Plastic-Bodied Locos	Tim Shackleton	Wild Swan	9781874103523	
Plastic Structure Kits	Ian Rice	Wild Swan	0906867711	A perfect accompaniment to the Wills range of structure kits
Railway Signalling and Track Plans	Bob Essery	Ian Allan	9780711032156	
Railway Stations from the Air	Aerofilms	Ian Allan	9780711029804	